"*Writer in a Life Vest* is a unique and utterly enchanting look at life in Washington state's San Juan Islands—a love letter to a specific area from a writer who clearly has a deep sense of place for her chosen home. A pleasure to read and hard to put down."

—DEBORAH GILES, PHD, Science and Research Director, Wild Orca

"Graville is so much more than a self-named 'storytelling lover of the Salish Sea.' This collection is an intimate investigation not from a dreamy-minded tourist, visiting journalist, or research scientist, but a writer-in-residence—by which I mean not just her brief writing residency on the Washington State Ferries system, but her decades-long residency on her island home, a writer deeply rooted in multiple dimensions of her ecosystem: above, below, and on the Salish Sea."

—HEATHER DURHAM, author of *Wolf Tree* and *Going Feral*

"Part personal reflection, part insightful commentary, all beautifully written ... Graville's essays foster a sense of place filled with wonder and hope—key ingredients for taking better care of the Salish Sea and all of us who depend on it."

—JOSEPH K. GAYDOS, Co-Author of the *The Salish Sea: Jewel of the Pacific Northwest*

"Witty, creative, insightful, and evocative, *Writer in a Life Vest* is passionate paean to the Salish Sea, ferry riding, and the creatures and people that inhabit this beautiful body of water. As the state's first writer-in-residence on a ferry, Iris Graville opens our eyes and hearts to the importance of caring for, paying attention to, and protecting the places we love."

—DAVID B. WILLIAMS, author of *Homewaters: A Human and Natural History of Puget Sound*

"The Salish Sea comes alive in this inspired collection of essays written by Iris Graville, who takes us on her journey through the San Juan Islands. Creatively woven together, we learn from these essays about the petition for a name change for the Salish Sea, and we discover the plight and the profound beauty of the Southern Resident Orcas. Most importantly, through Graville's poetry and narrative rhythm, we hear the alarm bell for each of us to take immediate action in today's climate crisis."

—KIP ROBINSON GREENTHAL, author of *Shoal Water*

"When a landscape makes a truth-claim on a human, blessed is s/he who hears, and heeds, it. In Iris Graville, the Salish Sea found a 'good and faithful servant' who devoted her time and talent to becoming the eyes, ears, and voice of the sea and its inhabitants. Through her imagination and writing skills, Graville succeeds in sharing both information and inspiration while bravely bearing witness on behalf of a beloved landscape. And we readers are the richer, and wiser, for it."

—GAIL COLLINS-RANADIVE, author of *Dinosaur Dreaming: Our Climate Moment*

"Mariners know the importance of safety at sea. We equip our vessels with emergency gear and watch our ship's instruments for hazards to navigation. In *Writer in a Life Vest*, Iris Graville alerts us to the dangers that threaten the safety of the sea itself. Every essay deepens our knowledge and love of these inland waters. Her words sound out a Mayday call to immediately begin a rescue of the Salish Sea."

—MIGAEL SCHERER, author *A Cruising Guide to Puget Sound*

"Graville writes through prose and poetry specifically of the Southern Resident orcas of the Salish Sea of Washington and British Columbia, but more generally of the climate crisis and how our actions today will affect all beings well into the future. Writer in a Life Vest is filled with wonder, tolerance, and sometimes brutal honesty, and peopled with the likes of Sylvia Earl, Greta Thunberg, and Rachel Carson. It stands as an ode on a ferry; a love song for the Salish Sea and all its inhabitants; and a carefully researched, heartfelt, deftly-written, and convincing plea to change what we can while we can."

—GENE HELFMAN, author of *Beyond the Human Realm*

Writer

in a

Life Vest

ESSAYS

FROM THE SALISH SEA

IRIS GRAVILLE

HOMEBOUND PUBLICATIONS

BERKSHIRE MOUNTAINS, MASS.

HOMEBOUND PUBLICATIONS

WWW.HOMEBOUNDPUBLICATIONS.COM

© 2022 TEXT BY IRIS GRAVILLE

The author has tried to recreate events, locales and conversations from her memories of them. In order to maintain their anonymity in some instances she has changed the names of individuals and places, she may have changed some identifying characteristics and details such as physical properties, occupations and places of residence.

Quantity sales. Special discounts are available on quantity purchases by associations, bookstores, and others. For details, contact the publisher or visit wholesalers such as Ingram.

All Rights Reserved
Published in 2022 by Homebound Publications
Cover Design by Leslie M. Browning
Interior Design by Jason Kirkey
Cover Image © Steve Horn
Map of the Salish Sea & Surrounding Basin, Stefan Freelan, WWU, 2009

ISBN 978-1-953340-48-1
First Edition Trade Paperback

10 9 8 7 6 5 4 3 2 1

Look for our titles in paperback, ebook, and audiobook wherever books are sold. Wholesale offerings for retailers available through Ingram.

Homebound Publications is committed to ecological stewardship. We greatly value the natural environment and invest in environmental conservation. For each book purchased in our online store, we plant one tree.

For Maggie

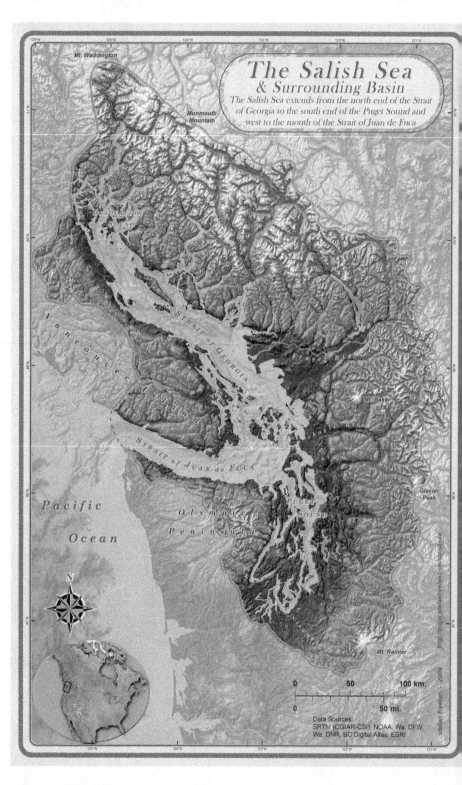

The Salish Sea
& Surrounding Basin

The Salish Sea extends from the north end of the Strait
of Georgia to the south end of the Puget Sound and
west to the mouth of the Strait of Juan de Fuca

Mt. Waddington

Monmouth
Mountain

DESOLATION
SOUND

STRAIT of GEORGIA

Fraser River

Mt. Baker

Vancouver Island

STRAIT of JUAN de FUCA

Glacier
Peak

Pacific

Ocean

Olympic
Peninsula

PUGET
SOUND

N

Mt. Rainier

0   50   100 km.

0   50 mi.

Data Sources:
SRTM (CGIAR-CSI), NOAA, Wa. DFW,
Wa. DNR, BC Digital Atlas, ESRI

http://maps.stefanfreelan.com/salishsea

stefan freelan · 2009

CONTENTS

ACKNOWLEDGMENT

of

AMERICA'S FIRST PEOPLES

I ACKNOWLEDGE I RESIDE on the ancestral lands and waters of Coast Salish peoples who have called this place home and cared for it from time immemorial. I wrote these essays on traditional lands and waters of Coast Salish tribes. I express my deepest respect and gratitude for these original and current caregivers and healers of this region.

I also acknowledge the disposition of Indigenous lands was often taken by coercive and violent acts and the disregard of treaties. I regret the harm done to First Nations people by colonizers, of which I'm a part. For that, I extend sincere apologies, and I pledge to work toward reconciliation.

INTRODUCTION

In our dream for the Salish Sea, we see a day when we all recognize and know our marine resources better than we now know corporate logos. We will watch and monitor the ecosystem better than we now watch the weather or monitor the NASDAQ or Dow Jones Industrial Average. And we will restore and protect the Salish Sea as if our lives and our livelihoods depend on it—because they do.

—AUDREY DELELLA BENEDICT
AND JOSEPH K. GAYDOS
The Salish Sea: Jewel of the Pacific Northwest

Growing up in Chicago and then smaller cities and tiny towns in the southern parts of Illinois and Indiana, I never imagined I'd someday live on an island in the Salish Sea. In fact, soon after moving from the Midwest to Seattle, I thought my husband's suggestion we visit the San Juan Islands meant a trip to the Caribbean! Yet, after nearly thirty years as an islander, I can't picture myself living anywhere but Lopez Island, one of 419 islands—most of them uninhabited—in the Salish Sea's San Juan Archipelago.

What power draws me to the Salish Sea? It's not just the water's satiny surface on a calm day or the racing white caps when the wind picks up. Part of the attraction is how the color shifts from almost black, to steel gray, to U.S.-flag blue, to, occasionally, the blue-green of the Mediterranean. Surely some of the lure is the way the inland water sweeps driftwood to the shore and swirls around bull kelp and sea grasses. Ebbs and floods soothe me, even as they pick up velocity and volume with tide changes. I'm always astounded by the majesty of pods of orcas gliding and diving in synchrony; or Harbor seals' rounded heads, blunt snouts, and brown eyes that pop up at my kayak's stern; or Steller sea lions sunbathing on barnacled rocks.

I attribute my love for the Salish Sea to all these individual features and more. But my true passion is for the way every lovely and fascinating part works with all the others in a latticework of life. Tide pools shelter herring eggs that hatch and feed minke whales. The Salish Sea gifts watershed forests with spawning Pacific salmon such as Chinook, coho, and sockeye—feasts for bears, bald eagles, ravens, and martens. Melting mountain snows glide into rivers which flow into wetlands, empty into bays, and swirl into the sea. The ocean connects to canals and lakes, and rivers on other continents, evaporates into clouds, and is filled by rain from skies around the globe. Some of those waters connect us by ferry and canoe, sailboats and transport vessels, carrying us and our goods, our cars and trucks, rice and coffee beans and, yes, oil.

Over the years, I've learned not just about what I love, but also about the perils that threaten this jewel. If we don't take care of the Salish Sea and all that contributes to it, the interwoven lattice of beauty, wildness, fragility, and relationship will collapse.

———

As an islander, I spend considerable hours on the Salish Sea, sometimes in a kayak, but primarily on the Washington State Ferries (WSF), the largest ferry system in the nation and third largest in the world. The fleet carries nearly twenty-five million people a year through some of the most majestic scenery on Earth.

While ferries are my connection to the mainland, the Interisland route travels among only four islands in the San Juans—Lopez, Shaw, Orcas, and San Juan. Over the years, that circuit has supplied time and space for me to write. During an outing with a friend on the Interisland in the spring of 2017, she recalled blog posts I'd written on the vessel during my twice-weekly commute to neighboring Orcas Island. For five years, I worked there as the school nurse. "One of my favorite blogs of yours," my friend volunteered, "was about riding the ferry." I wouldn't realize until later that her comment had lodged in my mind.

While I wrote short blog essays during my comings and goings to Orcas, I mostly worked on my third book, *Hiking Naked: A Quaker Woman's Search for Balance*. Homebound Publications published the memoir in the fall of 2017. As I offered readings and events to promote it, someone in the audience always asked, "What are you working on now?" I was clearer about what I *didn't* want to write—a sequel or anything else about myself—than what I did.

At the same time, my concerns about climate change in general, and the health of the Salish Sea in particular, grew. I wasn't alone: people throughout the islands and, indeed, the world, were becoming increasingly aware of the threat of ecological disasters. I'd studied the effects of warming waters and sea-level rise. I knew Southern Resident killer whales—also known as orca whales—neared extinction due to toxins and plastics in the water, vessel noise, and a 60 percent reduction in their main source of nutrition—Chinook salmon (the largest salmon, commonly known as "king" or "tyee"). I'd seen evidence of sea star wasting. I'd read that 30 percent of birds and 38 percent of mammals are listed as threatened, endangered, or candidates for these designations. I'd written agencies and government officials to urge them to prevent the risk of spills from increased oil transit. I became certain it was time to focus my writing on protecting and preserving the water and life that surrounded my home.

Doing some of that writing while drifting on the Salish Sea would undoubtedly influence and enhance my work. My friend's earlier praise likely stimulated thoughts of a yearlong writing residency on the Interisland ferry. As I considered the notion, it surfaced as a way to do my small part to protect this ferocious, fragile place. I "floated" the idea with a retired ferry boat captain and member of the Ferry Advisory Committee. He encouraged me to develop a proposal and submit it to a contact of his in the WSF system.

My proposal outlined the overall goal: a book-length collection of personal essays. I anticipated exploring history and details about the interisland route and the MV *Tillikum* (the vessel in service at that time for the Interisland circuit) and describing the Salish Sea and the effects of climate change on it and Southern Resident killer whales (SRKWS).

I didn't intend for the project to promote ferry ridership, though I expected it would be of interest to passengers. I also believed it could serve as another example of art collaborations of the WSF, such as the ferry schedule haiku competition and the longstanding tradition of art exhibits on ferries.

The structure of the interisland residency was simple. I planned to walk, not drive, onto the ferry on Lopez Island with my laptop, journal, and research materials and then ride, write, and read along the route. There would be no cost to me or the ferry system; the Interisland is the only route in the state system that allows walk-on passengers to ride free.

Although I hoped to interview crew members and passengers, I expected to devote most of my time to solitary writing and reading. And there would be plenty of time; another anomaly of this route is that walk-on passengers can ride from around six in the morning until eight at night (or later depending on the season) without ever disembarking until the vessel docks for the night at Friday Harbor on San Juan Island.

From August 1, 2018 until August 30, 2019, I served as the Washington State Ferries System's first writer-in-residence on the Interisland ferry. A crisp, white, table tent with my name in black lettering and the WSF logo in blue identified me and my role.

It took far longer than one term to complete this book, but many pieces had their beginnings at a table on the MV *Tillikum*, floating (sometimes pitching port to starboard) past rocky shorelines; snowy mountain ridges; forests of cedars, firs, and madrones; mansions and mobile homes. Seagull and eagle calls, briny wind currents, and tingling sea breezes stimulated my senses.

This is a collection of non-fiction essays, written not by a scientist or marine biologist, but by a storytelling lover of the Salish Sea. Most of the essays are in a form sometimes referred to as lyric, hybrid, collage, braided, or hermit crab—using existing forms as an outer covering to protect vulnerable, tender prose. You'll also find conversations, real and imagined, as well as the more traditional style of personal essays, like the one you're reading now.

In all of these creative nonfiction forms, I used techniques of both prose and poetry (language, imagery, sound, and rhythm) to explore topics I might not otherwise approach, and to lead readers to ask questions. I chose these styles as a metaphor for the new thinking I believe is an essential response to the climate crisis we're in. I offer them as symbols of resilience, inspiration, and hope.

The Tillikum

When anxious, uneasy, and bad thoughts come, I go to the sea, and the sea drowns them out with its great wide sounds, cleanses me with its noise, and imposes a rhythm upon everything in me that is bewildered and confused.

—RAINER MARIA RILKE

FERRY BOAT MEDITATION—
11/11/14

"Orcas Island. we're now arriving on Orcas Island."

The announcement startles me. Sitting in my Subaru on the ferry's car deck, I was absorbed in my writing meditation. I hadn't detected the boat slowing down, wasn't even aware the vessel had been moving. I look up from my computer, wedged between my lap and the steering wheel, to notice the jagged, black treetops on the shore outlined by the rising sun.

This is how I start my day twice a week. On these mornings, my pre-dawn meditation silence is broken by the voice of a ferry crew member. It's often Michael's pirate-like growl announcing our progress on the route to one of the neighboring islands where I work part-time as the school nurse. I never know what awaits me at the four hundred-student, k-12 campus. Lice? Anaphylactic reaction? Head injury on the playground? Between the wait in the Lopez Island ferry line to board and when I off-load at the run's second stop on Orcas Island, I steal forty-five minutes to quiet, center, pray, and write.

Here I type fast, ignoring typos and grammar, just trying to tap the words out as they flow from my solitary centering time. Often, like today, an idea comes to me that eventually ends up as a blog entry or an essay, and I capture the rough draft on my laptop.

It's not much time, but it's a start. No phone, no Internet, no piles of bills and correspondence to distract—just me, in the quiet of my car, with the boat's throbbing engine muffling other sounds.

I *could* leave the car and walk upstairs to the warmth of the passenger cabin and the quiet murmurings of other ferry commuters. I do that on some particularly cold mornings when the Subaru retains the night chill. But today, and most days, I decide instead to stay in this private meditation space and write my way closer to Spirit.

Michael's gravelly voice comes on the loudspeaker again. "Drivers and passengers, please return to your vehicles. Walk-ons depart from the car deck. This is Orcas Island."

I slide my cursor to the Save icon, direct my laptop to Shut Down, and breathe in and out deeply. An orange-vested crew member signals for me to drive off the deck and onto the Orcas Landing ramp. I pray these few minutes of solitude will sustain me through whatever the day brings until my ferry sanctuary returns me home.

WRITING SPACE AVAILABLE

(What an ad might look like for writers'
co-working space on the Interisland ferry.)

Writers, are you tired of writing in a windowless cubicle? Or in high rises blocking views of the outside world? Frustrated with having to ask for a key every time you want to use the restroom? Distracted by ringing phones and dinging message alerts?

If so, the *Motor Vessel* (MV) *Tillikum* could be just the place for you.

The MV *Tillikum* is the oldest vessel in the Washington State Ferries (WSF) fleet of twenty-nine boats in the state's "marine highways" network of ten ferry routes. This makes WSF the largest ferry system in the U.S. and the third-largest in the world. At 310 feet in length, the vessel can carry over one thousand passengers and eighty-seven vehicles. The vessel's name is Chinook dialect meaning friends, relatives, or tribe. Its gleaming white, steel exterior with smokestacks and wheelhouses trimmed in green is an iconic image of the Pacific Northwest (and *Grey's Anatomy* television series). It travels thirteen knots (about fifteen mph) as it cruises among four of the San Juan Islands: Lopez, Shaw, Orcas, and San Juan.

Launched in 1959 (when gas cost twenty-three cents per gallon and before Alaska became a state), the MV *Tillikum* retains some of the glamour of the 1950s, with its brass railings and alarm bells; green, leather swivel chairs (only a few rips on the seats) at a make-up table and mirror in the ladies' room (no key required to enter); and wooden slat benches at the bow and stern. Plaques commemorating the *Tillikum's* sixtieth birthday hang above the car deck on each end of the ferry; they'll remain until it's retired in 2022 at the age of sixty-three.

Here are other features that make the MV *Tillikum* an ideal writing office:

Rental Fees: None! No need for first and last month's rent as a deposit or monthly payment. You can walk on the *Tillikum* at no cost; it's the only route in the entire WSF system that doesn't charge passengers to ride.

Parking: It's free! All four island ferry terminals offer free parking if you drive to the ferry landing.

Entering Your Office Space: Although the ferry schedule changes seasonally, the *Tillikum* generally leaves its home berth in Friday Harbor at six a.m., makes five circles, and returns to Friday Harbor around eight-thirty p.m. Unloading vehicles and passengers and reloading require ten to fifteen minutes; you, however, can just stay on board while at the dock. Of course, you can board or disembark at any of the four islands.

Accessible Location: Loading ramps at all four ferry landings in the San Juans make boarding the *Tillikum's* car deck easy. "Walk-ons" go aboard before the cars, delivery trucks, and motorcycles, and there's no danger of being "overloaded." An elevator will take you to the main cabin, or you can add to your walking laps (see below) by climbing the stairs.

Versatile Internal Layout: Upholstered benches (long enough for the average person to stretch out for a nap) at each window; some seats include sturdy tables large enough for a laptop, books, and a travel mug and water bottle. Straight-back vinyl chairs with chrome armrests can be arranged in a variety of configurations in a large, open area; tables and red swivel chairs seat passengers in the galley. When the seas are calm, multiple scenic laps around the cabin can serve as your workout.

Proximity to Facilities: Separate bathrooms for men and women (see above) as well as an accessible, gender-neutral, private bathroom with a diaper-changing table. The galley on board is open during the daytime, serving hot and cold sandwiches, soup, coffee, tea, and cocoa, prepared salads, soft drinks, popcorn, and packaged cookies and candies. No ATM on board, but credit cards are accepted.

Comfortable Environment: Fluorescent lighting and ceiling heating/air conditioning do their best to create a comfortable workspace. Does the cabin feel stuffy? Step out on one of the decks and breathe in the pristine, briny air. You're on the Salish Sea, so polar fleece and socks are cozy accessories all year round. Noise levels are generally low, but you may flinch at occasional outbursts from youth commuting to school or sporting events on other islands, alarms for emergency drills, and voices over the loudspeaker announcing arrivals at islands. The (usually) gentle rocking of the boat offers a calming ride. Views through sea-sprayed windows will undoubtedly enhance your mental health and creativity: rocky shorelines dotted with chartreuse moss and lined with cedars, madrones, and firs; glacier-capped mountains in the distance; swooping gulls; and the occasional seal.

Co-tenants: You won't lack for companionship with the helpful and friendly crew and passengers (some of whom may be writers, too). And you never know when you'll be joined by a cello-playing truck driver, mahjong players, jugglers, or a Floating Ukulele Jam.

Internet & Phone Connection: What do you care? One of the main reasons you want this office is to escape the interruptions and disruptions of e-mail, social media, phone calls, texts, and googling, right? Unreliable cell service and the absence of free Internet are ideal for creative writing on the *Tillikum*. Although, if you must work online, access is available for a fee.

Unique Features: Your floating workspace includes elements you likely won't find in any other office. A few examples: surplus motor parts from a World War II destroyer; jigsaw puzzles on some tables that anyone can add to; a firefighting axe mounted in a red case on the wall; life vests stashed under seats; fire hoses with brass nozzles strategically placed throughout the cabin. It's not common, but you might possibly spot whales—minkes, Biggs, or Southern Resident killer whales.

The most important feature, though, is the places the ferry will take your thoughts, your wonder, and your imagination. The minute you settle into one of the booths on the *Tillikum*, you'll let go of worries and "to-do" lists. You'll notice your shoulders unknot; your brow unfurrows. Whether the sun turns the water a silvery blue, or winds whip it into swells, your concerns and checklists remain on shore, and the critic that resides on your shoulder becomes as still as a slack tide.

But don't take our word for it. Unfold a WSF schedule and turn to the departure and arrival times for the San Juan Islands. Review the highlighted sailings that indicate the Interisland route, and choose a time, any day of the week, that works for you. Welcome aboard the Washington State Ferries!

FRIENDS AND RELATIVES

Most passengers just refer to it as "the ferry." They know where it's headed, what time it departs the ferry terminal, and when it arrives at its destination. The name of the vessel isn't listed on the multi-fold, paper ferry schedule or on its online version through the Washington State Department of Transportation. If you look closely when you board, though, you'll find a small, wooden sign somewhere near the ferry's wheelhouse with the vessel's name carved on it. And some people take that name very seriously.

Washington State Ferries (WSF) are considered part of the state's highway network; the fleet of twenty-one vessels serves eight Washington counties as well as British Columbia, Canada. It's the Washington State Transportation Commission's (WSTC) responsibility to name these vessels as well as state highways and bridges. For ferries, state guidelines require the names have "statewide significance and represent Washington's image and culture," while avoiding "commercial overtones and anything offensive." Names of tribes, bodies of water, geographic locations, or terms that relate to nautical heritage meet those requirements.

While the criteria for ferry names are concise, the selection process is, well, not.

According to the WSTC, well in advance of a ferry naming, the agency issues a public request for names and describes deadlines and requirements. Once the date for name proposals has passed, the three Commissioners who serve as the "Ferry Team" review all submissions for compliance with established guidelines. Eligible options are sent to the Ferry Advisory Executive Council and the WSF, and they're posted on the WSTC website for review and input. If possible, the Ferry Riders Opinion Group (F.R.O.G.) will also be surveyed about the eligible names.

Upon completion of the above steps, eligible names are advanced to the seven-member WSTC along with all input received and a recommendation from the Ferry Team. The full Commission then selects the name.

It's possible this thorough process came about after the naming of two new vessels in 1958. According to sailing magazine "48° North" and the Saltwater People Historical Society, Lloyd Nelson, a member of the State Toll Bridge Authority, had been tasked with naming the new ferries in the state's then seven-year-old ferry system. The names he chose, perhaps influenced by the christening of the MV *Evergreen State* in 1954, were the *Vacation State* and the *Washington State*. A small item on a back page of the January 14, 1958 *Seattle Times* announced the names. Evidently, William O. Thorniley read the notice.

Thorniley, an employee of the private Black Ball Ferry Line before Washington State acquired it in 1951, was a long-time advocate of the use of Native American words for the ferries. When he learned about Nelson's proposed names, he enlisted the Seattle Chamber of Commerce to reject them. Over the next month, hundreds of citizens and newspapers joined in the debate, sending suggestions to the State Toll Bridge Authority. In the midst of the protest, Nelson withdrew his suggestions, and the state set up a nine-member committee, including Thorniley, to select names. After a three-month effort, one vessel was named *Klahowya*, meaning "greeting."

For the other ferry, the committee selected *Tillikum*. The word is Chinook jargon, with elements from Chinook, Nootka, English, French, and other languages that means "friends and relatives."

The oldest ferry operating in the wsf system, and the sole remaining Evergreen State-class ferry, the MV *Tillikum's* history is even more complex and convoluted than its naming process. Built in 1959 to carry one thousand passengers and one hundred vehicles, the *Tillikum* first sailed between Seattle and Bainbridge Island.

As the population boomed in the Puget Sound region, a larger and faster Super-class ferry was designed to supplement the small Evergreen State-class models. In 1968, the Super-class MV *Kaleetan* replaced the *Tillikum,* which moved to the Edmonds-Kingston run. In the early 1980s, the *Tillikum* was displaced by the Issaquah-class ferry, MV *Chelan.* Next, she became a relief boat for nearly a decade until she settled on the Fauntleroy-Vashon-Southworth run in the early 1990s. Rebuilt in 1994, the *Tillikum* became a reserve vessel until her sister, *Klahowya,* retired in 2017. That's when the *Tillikum* became the San Juan Islands' interisland vessel, where she remains today.

Chapter One in *Orca: Shared Waters, Shared Home* (Braided River, 2021) by *Seattle Times* journalist Lynda V. Mapes, is titled "The People That Live Under the Sea." It includes a story told by the late Bill James, hereditary chief of the Lummi people, of how they believe the orcas are related to them. With that creation story as a backdrop, Mapes describes the plight of the orcas, or, as the Lummi call them, the blackfish. She writes specifically of the Southern Resident orcas and how the "human and orca cultures of the Salish Sea have shared these waters for thousands of years. And like the Lummi and other Coast Salish communities, the Southern Resident orca families share customs, culture, language, a deep knowledge of the water, and food."

From Mapes's reporting, it's easy to conclude that Coast Salish words are the language of the Salish Sea. So it's fitting that now, with the exception of the MV *Rhododendron,* all current wsf vessels have tribal names. They include:

- *Chelan* from the word Tsillan for "deep water,"
- *Sealth* for Suquamish and Duwamish Chief Sealth, after whom the City of Seattle was named,

- *Tokitae*, Coast Salish dialect for "nice day, pretty colors, "
- *Kittitas*, the tribe of "shoal people" who lived along the shallow portion of the Yakima River near Ellensburg, also defined as "land of bread."

And, though it took many years for the *Tillikum* to make her way to the daily circuit among the San Juan Islands, she is now among friends and relatives.

NOT JUST A DRILL

There is a terribly terrestrial mindset about what we need to do to take care of the planet—as if the ocean somehow doesn't matter or is so big, so vast that it can take care of itself, or that there is nothing that we could possibly do that we could harm the ocean.

—SYLVIA EARLE,
oceanographer and marine biologist

Once a week, a ferry crew member announces, "In a few moments, we'll ring alarm bells. This is just a drill, not an actual emergency."

If I'm writing on the Interisland ferry during a drill, I glance at posters in the ferry cabin. They identify passenger assembly stations at each end of the vessel and carry sobering, emergency messages. No matter how often I read them, I pause, reminded I might need to follow the directions sometime.

EMERGENCIES
"Go to the nearest Passenger Assembly Stations whenever you hear an emergency signal. It is important for your own safety that you follow the directions you are given. Please notify the crew if you have any special training that may be of use during an emergency."

During this time of climate chaos, many of us create our own assembly stations. We gather in living rooms and around kitchen tables. We plan protests, devise strategies to be fossil-fuel-free, and write letters to government leaders and corporate executives. We seek out those with special training and learn from them how to be of use during emergencies like oil tanker spills and sick or dying orcas. Some of us assemble on sacred grounds, in kayaks on the Salish Sea, and at climate conferences. We can no longer deny this is an emergency.

LIFE JACKETS
"Obtain a life jacket from a designated life jacket locker, underneath a bench seat, or from a crew member. Life jacket locations are clearly marked throughout the vessel. Put on life jackets as instructed by crew-members. Adults should make sure that children are correctly fitted with their life jackets."

By ignoring alarms sounded about coal, fracking, endangered owls and orcas and coral reefs, overdevelopment, and overpopulation, we've failed to ensure our children (and grandchildren) won't need life jackets. Now, thousands of teens like Greta Thunberg of Sweden are instructing us. Their message? "Stop denying, the earth is dying. The seas are rising, and so are we."

HYPOTHERMIA PROTECTION
"The crew will instruct passengers about hypothermia prevention and cold-water survival techniques."

Hypothermia is still a threat in the Salish Sea as global ocean temperatures rise. But survival techniques? Those, we need.

ABANDON SHIP

"Seven short rings, followed by one long ring on the general alarm bells signal to abandon ship. Upon hearing the abandon ship signal, go immediately to a Passenger Assembly Station. This order will only be given if the Captain is certain it is safer for you in a life raft than aboard the ferry. When the order to abandon ship is given, the crew will direct you to calmly and quickly move to the designated Embarkation Stations on the car deck. They represent the locations where you would leave the vessel."

We've been hearing alarm bells for Earth for decades, at least since 1962 when *Silent Spring* author Rachel Carson warned us of the hazards of the pesticide, DDT. Eyewitness stories, movies about inconvenient truths, and scientific reports make grave predictions about dying rainforests; melting glaciers; rising sea levels; more frequent, catastrophic hurricanes and wildfires; and disappearing species. While I appreciate the ferry crew's weekly drills to prepare for emergencies, the truth is, these climate projections pose much greater threats to our safety.

Earth's oceans, rivers, air, drinking water, forests, and soil constantly sound short and long rings. An Abandon Earth signal, however, is not an option. There are no Embarkation Stations. There's nowhere a life raft can take us.

We've stayed calm for too long. It's time to move quickly.

This is not just a drill.

JAMMIN' ON THE SALISH SEA

The third Thursday in May, shortly after the MV *Tillikum* departed from Orcas Island, twangs and plunks masked the usual rumble of the ferry's engine. Fifteen passengers tuned ukuleles, banjeleles (ukulele neck on a banjo body), and guitars. I'd scheduled my ferry-writing-and-riding time in the late afternoon that day, precisely to witness the monthly Ukulele Jam.

A ukulele-playing friend from Orcas Island had alerted me to the get-together and encouraged me to ride along—even though I've never played any kind of stringed instrument. The first arrivals scoped out the end of the vessel where chairs can be moved into a circle. At each island, people toting instrument cases made their way to the gathering, with the largest number boarding at Orcas. One of them, Anita, filled me in about the origins and history of this one-year-old group.

Anita's husband, Gordon, had tried to organize a monthly ukelele jam on Orcas, but the place he'd hoped to hold it didn't work out. "He was trying to come up with something else," Anita said. As often happens in the islands, a bit of serendipity nurtured the idea of a *floating* uke jam. "I commute to Shaw on foot to teach music lessons once a week," Anita said, "hauling a guitar, uke, mandolin, and sometimes a hand saw." (I've heard Anita play the "singing saw" with Orcas Island's Olga Symphony. The sound she creates is ethereal). It's hard to miss Anita with her collection of instruments, and over the years she's become known to the ferry workers.

"One night on my way home from the mainland," she said, "a ferry worker came up to me and said he'd heard there's a guy on Orcas planning to put together a ukulele jam." Anita explained it was her husband who wanted to organize the music. The crew member asked Anita to keep him posted about it. "I'd love to come some time," he said.

"You know, it's too bad we can't do the jam on the ferry," Anita said. "Then I thought, wait a minute ... why not? Especially the free-to-walk-on, friendly-crew Interisland. And the idea was hatched." When she pitched it to Gordon, he was game to try.

The first floating jam took place in June 2018. "The third Thursday is the regular date," Anita said, "because it's so nicely alliterative and therefore easy to remember." The range of experience among the players seemed varied, and I asked Anita if all levels are welcome. "Totally!" she replied. "We even had a couple of women who happened to be on board for the first float, got inspired, went out and got ukes, and joined us the next month!"

Anita encourages people to come and play when they can and sing when they can't. "Down the road, they'll find they can play more and more." She also urges her students to join in. "It's so good and important to play with others ... and fun!"

The evening I rode, many of the "jammers" brought music stands and sheet music to share. Someone called out, "'Pancho and Lefty' in the key of G." As the jam progressed, others suggested folk songs, waltzes, and ballads, including "Wildflowers," "The Wild Rover," "Skye Boat Song," and "Ring of Fire." A man and woman outside the circle of musicians tapped their toes and swayed to the music. When the group played "Don't Worry, Be Happy," their feet slid into dance steps.

Anita noted, "Passengers love it. We've had people get on just to listen to the music and watch the scenery. I guess there might be plenty who don't like it, but they just go to the other end of the boat, so we don't know about them."

So far, the uke players have had only one special event—a Jammie Jam. "I had to work on the third Thursday of December last year," Anita recalled, "so we moved the gathering to Sunday. One of the Shaw folks suggested we wear pajamas—they go to bed early on Shaw— so..." That night, viola and keyboard players also joined the pajama-clad group.

I never made it to another jam on the Interisland, and it might be another year or two before the gatherings resume due to COVID-19. When they do, I hope to join the group again for some "don't worry, be happy" time. And who knows, maybe someday I'll be tempted to try the uke myself.

LIKE CUTTING
THROUGH BUTTER

The Washington State Ferries (wsf) System is looking ahead—twenty years ahead, as a matter of fact. In 2019, with copies of the department's draft *2040 Long-Range Plan* in hand, staff made the rounds of ferry-served communities and the vessels themselves. They previewed some of the plans on the Interisland during one of my writing times. Sadly, the plan requires decommissioning older vessels, and my beloved MV *Tillikum* is slated to be the next to retire in 2022.

Don't get me wrong, I'm thrilled wsf is exploring ways to improve service reliability and "green the fleet." Two Executive Orders in 2019 directed wsf to "begin the transition to a zero-carbon-emission ferry fleet" and to "explore strategies to quiet ferries to protect the struggling orca whale population."

But, I admit, I'll miss some of the unique characteristics of the *Tillikum* when she goes into mothballs. The vessel features a number of design elements common to the 1950s when she was built. I'm charmed by the amount of brass on board and the wooden slat benches on the bow and stern. And she's the only vessel I've seen with a make-up table and swivel chairs in the "Ladies' Room."

———

One week, my regular writer-in-residence time found me boarding the *Salish*. The crew said the *Tillikum* was in Seattle for her "annual checkup." The *Salish* is a lovely vessel and one I've ridden in the past on her usual Coupeville-to-Port Townsend route.

Like the *Tillikum* and many other ferries in the system, the *Salish* showcases traditional prints by Coast Salish artists and landscape photos by regional photographers. The day I rode, I noticed the crew had left jigsaw puzzles on tables, just like on the *Tillikum*.

Still, she *wasn't* the *Tillikum*. We regulars felt disoriented on the smaller vessel (she carries only sixty-four vehicles, compared to the *Tillikum's* eighty-seven vehicle capacity). This "youngster" (she's only been in service eight years) just doesn't have the same allure as the sixty-year-old *Tillikum*.

I was comforted to learn, however, that while the *Tillikum* was in Seattle for repairs, she had a party. Friends of the ferry, including crew, engineers, and maintenance workers, unveiled commemorative emblems to recognize the vessel's six decades of service. The *Tillikum* began her career on the Seattle-Bainbridge run, and she's operated on nearly all ten routes in the system. Washington State Ferries Assistant Secretary Amy Scarton presented two plaques to be installed above the car deck on each end of the ferry—a first for the ferry system.

———

Regardless of the *Tillikum's* history, the crew and I (and likely many other islanders) think of her as "our ferry." Chief Mate Donna Tegnell has worked her way from the deck to the pilothouse. She sums up her love for the vessel: "She has a beautiful keel, and when it comes to docking, it's like cutting through butter." Donna says the crew hopes the *Tillikum* stays on the Interisland route until her retirement.

Speaking of butter, just a week after the *Tillikum's* anniversary commemoration, she returned "home" in time for one passenger to celebrate her own birthday on board with a piece of pastry. "I wish I were as 'young' as the *Tillikum*," the woman said, after blowing out her birthday candle.

———

I know a quieter, more fuel-efficient vessel will ply the waters of the Salish Sea when the *Tillikum* goes out of service. The interior undoubtedly will be different, too. But, some of the vessel's most important characteristics will stay the same—the helpful and friendly crew, the calming ride, and the inspiring views.

Writer-in-Residence

Don't try to figure out what other people want to hear from you; figure out what you have to say. It's the one and only thing you have to offer.

—BARBARA KINGSOLVER

RES·I·DENT

rez(ə)dənt, noun
1 a person who lives somewhere permanently or on a long-term basis: *Lopez Island is a beautiful hamlet with two thousand, five hundred year-round residents.* **2** a bird, butterfly, or other animal of a species that does not migrate: *Southern Resident killer whales are found mostly off the coasts of British Columbia, Washington, California, and Oregon.*
idiom: in residence Committed to live and/or work in a specific place, often for a certain length of time: *Iris was the first writer-in-residence for the Washington State Ferries.*

Being "in residence" offers writers time and space for creativity and productivity. Writing residencies are available in nearly every state in the U.S.— from mansions to cabins located in forests, atop mountains, alongside rivers, on working farms, and in buzzing cities. You can find them in countries around the globe including France, China, Mexico, and Iceland.

Well-known, long-established U.S. writing residencies such as Bread Loaf, Hedgebrook, and the MacDowell Colony—to name a few—offer meals, housing, and stipends to cover expenses. They're highly competitive, with far more applicants every year than available slots. These residencies also require relocating for weeks, months, or even an entire year. Other locations with less stringent admission requirements typically cost hundreds to thousands of dollars for room and board plus transportation.

In recent years, some writers have pursued unique alternatives to boost focus and inspiration.

Since 2011, Amtrak has offered writers' residencies on trains, particularly long-distance routes. Writers are drawn to the gentle movement of the train, the ever-changing scenery, passenger conversations, and freedom from timelines and expectations for up to a week.

To celebrate the fiftieth anniversary of Seattle's Space Needle in 2012, journalist Knute Berger became writer-in-residence there to research and gather stories for his book, *Space Needle: The Spirit of Seattle*. Every Thursday throughout the spring and summer, Berger wrote 520 feet above ground on the landmark's observation deck. He'd been fascinated by "the Needle" since 1961, when, as an eight-year-old Cub Scout, he saw it under construction.

Applications overwhelmed the City of Seattle in 2016 when it advertised for the first writer-in-residence at the iconic Fremont Bridge. The drawbridge swings upward for marine traffic about thirty-five times a day. Its hundredth birthday in 2017 coincided with the three-month paid position. The City selected author Elissa Washuta, a member of the Cowlitz Indian tribe, and from June through August 2016, the bridge's northwest tower served as her residency studio. The eight- by thirteen-foot space with a ten-foot ceiling was furnished with a desk, a chair, overhead lights, and windows that gave Washuta 360-degree views of the surrounding area. "White City," an essay based on the history of Puget Sound, including the lives of First Peoples, the creation of Seattle's waterways for commerce and industry, and rapid change in the city, resulted from her in-depth exploration of the bridge.

I became the first-ever writer-in-residence for the Washington State Ferries System in August 2018, a role I developed and proposed to the agency. Once or twice a week, I walked aboard the MV *Tillikum* (also known as the Interisland), the vessel that routes passengers around the San Juan Islands. I'd carry my sloshing coffee mug, my backpack filled with books, journals, and my laptop. The Interisland leaves its home berth in Friday Harbor on San Juan Island each morning around six a.m. and makes five circles to Orcas, Shaw, and Lopez before returning to Friday Harbor at eight-thirty p.m.

Once I boarded the Interisland from my home on Lopez—known as "The Friendly Isle" because locals wave to all passing vehicles—I rarely debarked, even though at times I was tempted. Each island has its own personality, landscape, and attractions.

My first stop was Shaw, the smallest of the ferry-served islands. It's quiet and pastoral, with no commercial businesses except for a small store at the ferry landing. Orcas, the largest geographically, offers varied landscapes of pastures, forests, and beaches. Mt. Constitution, rising nearly a half-mile above sea level on Orcas, is the highest point in the San Juan Islands. There's plenty of commerce on Orcas, just as there is on San Juan Island, home to Friday Harbor, the islands' only incorporated town and the county seat.

It typically takes ten to fifteen minutes for the ferry to off-load vehicles and passengers and re-load at each landing; I just stayed on board while at the dock. There was plenty to see and do at all the stops, but I was there to write.

My "office" measured 310 feet in length, could carry over a thousand passengers and eighty-seven vehicles and traveled thirteen knots (about fifteen mph) as it cruised. Throughout my one-year term, I usually sat on the passenger deck in a booth with a table and a 180-degree view of the Salish Sea, one of the world's largest inland seas.

The sea straddles the international border between Washington State and British Columbia, Canada, and includes inland marine waters of the Strait of Juan de Fuca, Puget Sound, and the Strait of Georgia plus the southern end of Vancouver Island, the San Juan Islands, the Gulf Islands, and smaller islands. It's a seascape of deep fjords, rocky islands, sheltered bays and inlets, and lush estuaries nourished by networks of braided rivers.

For me, this residency offered a change of pace; a change of scenery; and a break from distractions in my home office such as bills, "to do" lists, household chores, and the telephone (cell coverage is spotty on board). Much like Amtrak, the motion of the ferry soothed and invigorated me, depending on how calm or jarring the seas.

Only a few people interrupted my work on my residency days. I guess my head bent over my laptop with my eyes fixed on the screen indicated, "Do Not Disturb." Other Salish Sea residents, however, would have received much more attention, had they appeared. During the decades I've traveled by ferry, I've spotted orca whales near the vessels only a few times. I'd hoped they'd swim by during my residency, but that wasn't to be. The Interisland route isn't the whales' usual course through this waterway; they prefer more open passages in the Straits of Juan de Fuca and Georgia. It's also possible they're avoiding the noise of vessel traffic that makes hunting for dwindling king salmon more difficult. It remains to be seen if these endangered residents continue to find the nourishment they need from the Salish Sea.

As the end of my term— August 30, 2019—approached, I began the search for a successor. I reviewed the twenty applications I received and then recruited a small committee of writers to read the five I considered the strongest (no easy task, as they were all high quality). We all agreed, however, that Liz Smith from San Juan Island was our top choice to serve as the 2020 writer-in-residence. Her tenure was cut short due to COVID-19's travel restrictions, so she plans to resume the role sometime in 2021. Hopefully, many more residents—writers and whales—will follow her.

WRITER IN A LIFE VEST

A crew member called out as the *Tillikum* sat in the berth in Friday Harbor after all the passengers had disembarked. "The writer is still on board," she said.

"It's *Iris*," another replied, "*Iris* is the writer."

I left the table where I usually wrote on the ferry to find crew-members Teri and Suzanne discussing my presence.

"We're gonna have a fire drill," Suzanne said. "Just wanted to warn ya."

A few seconds later, a bell sounded—a long jangle lower in tone than a classic telephone ring and about ten decibels louder. I returned to my writing spot to watch what would unfold. Teri trotted to a passenger bench near the outdoor deck and lifted the vinyl-covered seat. She pulled two orange life vests from the stash and walked toward me.

"You can be my guinea pig," she said, handing me one of the vests. As she donned the other, she instructed me to loosen the side straps on mine, remove my glasses, slide the vest over my head, and tug the straps for a snug fit.

"If you ever have to jump into the water," she explained, "hold onto the top of the vest so it doesn't ride up, and cross your legs at the ankles."

I gulped, then mimicked her actions in the cabin as I watched a spray of water shoot out of a fire hose over the ferry's port side.

"Bring your knees to your chest to conserve energy," Teri continued. "Or if you see a log, you could drape your knees over it." I nodded silently and swallowed again.

After Teri took a photo, I removed the bright, uncomfortable lifesaving equipment, grateful this was only a drill. Wearing that vest, I felt a combination of peril and protection. Three shorter, echoing jangles signaled the drill's conclusion.

"If we have a real emergency," Teri said, "you can help."

As I returned to my desk, Suzanne strode through the cabin, dressed in full firefighting gear—yellow helmet with a plastic face shield; bulky, yellow jacket and pants; thick gloves; and black boots. She'd been wielding the fire hose on the upper deck.

"We do these drills once a week," she explained, perspiration glistening her face.

I thought of the varied kinds of vulnerability Teri, Suzanne, and I can feel in our work. *They* put their lives at risk when there's a fire or some other emergency on board. When I write, particularly personal essays, *my* risk is different—but present, nonetheless. Often, my heart feels especially unprotected—as if it's covered with only the thinnest layer of skin and no sternum. Most writers I know describe the same sense of baring heart and soul.

Every time I wrote on the *Tillikum* or in my home office, fears about the imperiled Salish Sea stalked me. The deaths in 2018 of two Southern Resident orcas—J50 (Scarlet) and a calf born to J35 (Tahlequah)—brought worldwide attention to the impact of pollution, noise, and diminishing food sources on these mammals. Tahlequah gave birth to a healthy male calf, J57 (Phoenix), in September 2020; however, the mortality rate for infants is fifty percent due to high levels of toxins in whale mothers' breast milk. Like the spotted owl—endangered by over-harvesting old-growth forests—the potential extinction of orca whales demands protection by humans as well as a halt to our damaging behaviors.

I'm no marine biologist, but I'm compelled to use my art to write about the sea, the threats to its survival, and the protection measures many people resist. Still, I couldn't help asking myself whether I had the authority to write about these issues.

Sometimes I've yearned for a bulletproof vest like actor Nathan Fillion's in the television show, *Castle*. Fillion played Rick Castle, a novelist and part-time detective with NYPD. Whenever Castle joined the "real" detectives on a criminal investigation, he zipped up a black vest emblazoned with the word WRITER in white letters. After the fire drill on the ferry, I recalled the snug fit of that life vest and imagined it giving me the confidence to expose my beliefs, fears, angers, and joys on the page.

We're in a real emergency, and Teri said I could help.

The truth is, the climate crisis endangers everyone, and we all need metaphorical life vests. I hope mine will sustain me to foster hope and give me the courage to speak. Southern Resident whales, Chinook/king salmon, rockfish, anemones, urchins, sea stars, puffins, marbled murrelets … they're as desperate for life vests as we are.

NINE WAYS TO WRITE ON THE FERRY WHEN YOU'RE THE WRITER-IN-RESIDENCE

1. **Sit**. Place a folded sign with your name and title on the table where you usually work. A table under sepia photographs of Coast Salish peoples rocking a baby in a cradleboard, carving wood, and hunting whales. Some of their faces carry deep creases; many fold chapped and worn hands in their laps. They lived, worked on, and cared for this sea long before you did, years before this sixty-year-old vessel plied these waters at 13 knots, coursing between islands that now carry names of European explorers who claimed them as their own.
2. **Scrawl.** With a pen in a leather, handbound journal, numbering each page and dating each entry. Record conversations overheard; observations of rocky cliffs, cedars, and coppery Madrones; and jewel-like water carrying the 310-foot *Tillikum* on its route through Washington's San Juan Islands.
3. **Type.** On a shiny, 13-inch, three-pound laptop Coast Salish tribes never could have imagined. Nor European explorers.

43

Nor you when you first learned to type on a black, Royal type-writer, followed by a cranberry, IBM self-correcting electric typewriter, your reward when you could tap out 50 words per minute. Sometimes, type on a smartphone to preserve unexpected bits of conversation, possible essay topics, names and contact information of people who know so much more than you about ferries, the sea, orca whales, harbor seals, kingfishers and cormorants, kelp, starfish, jellyfish, Chinook salmon, and how the water can wear dozens of colors during a single sweep of the interisland route.

4. **Breathe**. On a wooden bench in the covered, outdoor deck, wind whistling through the open sides, rain spattering the square windows overlooking the uncovered deck where other passengers huddle. Fingerless gloves allow you to grip your pen until your digits stiffen and redden, and sea spray blurs the ink on the page.

5. **Linger**. In the Galley, enveloped by smells of fake-butter popcorn under a heat lamp, clam chowder simmering in a pot, and coffee when a passenger pumps the thermos top and stirs in cream and sugar. Banter in your preschool-level Spanish with Juan when you pay him for your coffee. Notice his eyes glisten and his hands cover his heart when a Costa Rican CD plays his favorite tune.

6. **Revise**. Insert ear buds to signal you're deep in thought and not desiring conversation. Or perhaps you're lost in daydreaming or fretting over words that don't come to describe images, fears, hopes, and wonder. Some days, many days, are like that, just a few worthy words saved in the journal or the laptop's memory.

7. **Walk**. Close the laptop lid or the leather journal. You've read that walking stimulates creativity. Stroll to the outside deck as the ferry docks. Let your eyes follow walk-on passengers with dogs on leashes; cyclists in spandex and cleats pushing their bikes; paddlers in sandals hefting kayaks; then the stream of cars, vans, gravel trucks, lumber trucks, pickups pulling trailers with horses, sheep, goats, or cows; Sysco and beer trucks;

sometimes a school bus or an ambulance, or motor homes. You know they all have stories.

8. **Read**. Instructions about what to do if there's a fire on the ferry or if passengers need to prepare to unexpectedly exit. Historical information about the Washington State Ferries. Posters about bike rides, fun runs, concerts, and how to protect the Salish Sea. Framed certificates for captains, first mates, and engineers. Plaques recognizing the crew's safety records and customer service. Brochures for tourists about where to sleep, eat, drink, shop, hike, and watch whales. Read books of poetry and essays you stashed in your backpack for inspiration. Read, because reading is essential to writing.

9. **Nap**. After a morning of reading and writing, then lunch, return to the pen or the keyboard until you notice letters turning into loops and trailing off the page, or typos appearing on the screen, or your eyelids fluttering and your neck bobbing. Don't resist these signs to rest. Succumb to the ferry's cradle-like motion, and nap, trusting you'll be roused by Ordinary Seaman Michael's raspy announcement, Lowwwwwpez…Lopez Island." As you leave, notice a vase of lilacs Able-bodied Seaman Teri cut from her garden.

WSF SONG

But did he ever return? No, he never returned
And his fate is still unlearned
He may ride forever 'neath the streets of Boston
He's the man who never returned.

—JACQUELINE STEINER &
BESS LOMAX HAWES
"MTA Song"*

Well, let me tell you a story 'bout a writer named Iris
Who boarded the ferry one wintry morn.
She wrote and she wrote until the third island stop
When she started to feel a bit worn.

Will she ever return? Oh, will she ever return?
For her Lopez home she'll yearn.
She may ride forever 'round the San Juan Islands,
The writer who never returned.

She didn't pay a fare, walking on and off is free,
And she could ride and write all day,
But at San Juan Island she was feeling pretty hungry,
So, she trudged to the Bean Café.

Will she ever return? Oh, will she ever return?
For her Lopez home she'll yearn.
She may ride forever 'round the San Juan Islands,
The writer who never returned.

A waiter told the writer, while she lunched at the Bean,
"Ice has frozen the Lopez dock!"
Then the writer's heart skipped several beats
As she felt a wave of shock.

Will she ever return? Oh, will she ever return?
For her Lopez home she'll yearn.
She may ride forever 'round the San Juan Islands,
The writer who never returned.

The Washington State Ferries sent an email alert
That repairs would likely take all night,
So, Iris called some friends on San Juan Island,
The kind souls prepared a bed and bite.

Will she ever return? Oh, will she ever return?
For her Lopez home she'll yearn.
She may ride forever 'round the San Juan Islands,
The writer who never returned.

A midnight alert said the Lopez dock was working,
and a ferry would be coming right by.
So, her friends drove her to the boat
and she let out a grateful sigh.

Will she ever return? Oh, will she ever return?
For her Lopez home she'll yearn.
She may ride forever 'round the San Juan Islands
The writer who never returned.

Now you island dwellers who travel by ferry,
Don't forget you must come prepared.
Pack a toothbrush and chargers for all your devices
In case your vessel becomes impaired.

Will she ever return? Oh, will she ever return?
For her Lopez home she'll yearn.
She may ride forever 'round the San Juan Islands
The writer who never returned.

One week later, snowfall covered the islands
But the ferries continued to churn.
Iris took another chance as Writer-in-Residence.
She's the writer who always returns.

Will she ever return? Oh, will she ever return?
For her Lopez home she'll yearn.
She may ride forever 'round the San Juan Islands
The writer who never returned.

* "MTA Song" appeared in 1956 as a campaign song for the Progressive Party candidate for mayor of Boston, Walter O'Brien. It was written in protest of the proposed fare increase requiring riders to pay on entering and again on leaving the subway. A version of the song, with the candidate's name changed, became a 1959 hit when recorded by American folk-singing group, The Kingston Trio. *The song inspired me to salute the* WSF (*Washington State Ferries*) *as well as the Lopez and San Juan dock crews, the Bean Café, and friends on San Juan Island. They all kept me from being "the writer who never returned." I was back a week later, better prepared for delays—that never occurred.*

WRITERS ON BOARD

"Do ferry passengers interrupt your writing to talk?" I received this question about my writing residency more times than I can remember. The writer-in-residence table tent sign I set out while writing was an invitation for inquiries, and I found those conversations fruitful. I chatted with a whale researcher, an environmental sciences professor who offered to send me reports, a cello-playing delivery truck driver, a priest, a group of mah jong players, and numerous crew members. Other writers were the most intrigued; with them I had supportive discussions about the joys and challenges of writing.

One of those meetings turned into a friendship when Elizabeth, a fellow writer from Orcas Island, introduced herself. "I do this, too," she said, explaining she often rides on the ferry as she writes science fiction and fantasy with romance. "Maybe we could write together sometime." A liaison for National Novel Writing Month (NaNoWriMo), Elizabeth had been organizing writing events in the San Juan Islands. We exchanged business cards and soon were emailing to set up a time for shared writing times (write-ins) on the Interisland route.

NaNoWriMo, a nonprofit formed in 1999, challenges writers to complete the first draft of a novel during the thirty days of November. In 2017, over 300,000 writers around the world participated. Elizabeth has been among them several times and committed to draft her second novel in November 2019. She decided to seek support and camaraderie with other islanders by organizing write-ins at coffee shops, libraries, or anywhere writers wanted to meet.

I have no aspirations to write a novel; in fact, writing fiction daunts me. But as a nonfiction writer for nearly twenty-five years, I know how helpful it can be to gather with others, regardless of their genres, and write together. Elizabeth and I suspected a write-in on the ferry might inspire others with the same goal, so we scheduled one for the second week of November. Elizabeth took it from there, inviting writers to join us.

I boarded first, on Lopez, and wrote alone during the twenty-minute sailing to Orcas, where Elizabeth and two other writers joined me in my booth. Essential writing tools covered the table—laptops, notebooks, and chocolate. While NaNoWriMo has a standard format for write-ins, we determined we were NaNoWriMo "rebels," each following what works best for us and our specific projects. Forty minutes later, the ferry stopped at San Juan, and another writer made us a group of five, divided between two booths.

One way NaNoWriMo helps is that it "tracks words for writers like Fitbit tracks steps for the ambulatory." After nearly three hours circling the islands, we each tallied our respective word counts. Collectively, our time together that day yielded 38,087 words of fiction written, one novel seriously pondered, and two essays revised. We concluded NaNoWriMo needs to add ferries to its list of recommended sites for writing.

A couple of months later, another group of writers joined me on board. All had been awarded week-long Artist Residency Fellowships on Orcas Island. The residencies, offered by Orcas Artsmith, provide time and space for writers to create new works. Four Fellows, along with Artsmith founder/author/publisher Jill

McCabe Johnson, wrote with me for several hours. All accomplished writers, they inspired me with the range of projects they were working on: a memoir; a poetry collection about clear-cutting an urban forest; a travel memoir; and essays about living as neighbors with elk and bear in a Seattle suburb. Jill was at work, too, "tinkering with an essay collection about maps and wayfinding. But it's a big, tumultuous mess right now," she admitted.

Jill couldn't have known what a comfort her words were to me as I muddled through early drafts for this essay collection. Surrounded by other writers, brows furrowed as they tapped keyboards and scribbled in notebooks, I felt heartened to keep at it.

As my one-year term as writer-in-residence neared its end, a small committee selected Liz Smith from San Juan Island to serve as the 2020 Writer-in-Residence. Liz grew up in the San Francisco Bay Area and has lived and traveled far and wide, pursuing her interests at the intersection of science, culture, and the environment. She planned to be in the residency "office" on the ferry at least once a week as she juggled several writing projects.

Soon after her appointment, I joined Liz for a day of writing on the Interisland. That time, she was the one with a table tent. When we wrote together, she was finishing the script for a PBS "Changing Seas" episode about the Deepwater Horizon oil spill cleanup. She'd also been working on the forthcoming feature film, YOUTH V GOV. That documentary is the story of twenty-one plaintiffs, now ages twelve to twenty-three, who sued the U.S. government for its "willful actions in creating the climate crisis they [the youth] will inherit." Waiting on her writing desk at home were a non-fiction book about using media and film to create change in the world and a novel about a young girl finding her own power in the midst of the climate crisis. Liz says, "I'm interested in fiction that's more hopeful—people adapting to climate change; there's not enough written about the fixing part."

A few months into Liz's time as writer-in-residence, the COVID-19 pandemic interfered. Throughout 2020, physical distancing decreased the number of seats available on the ferry's passenger deck; non-essential travel was discouraged and, at times, banned. As the end of Liz's original term approached in August 2020, she agreed to resume the role as soon as it's safe and to continue as the resident writer until August 2021.

When the pandemic loses its punch, I hope to rejoin Liz and other writers. After a year (and counting) of solitary work in my home office, I yearn for the camaraderie writing on board offers.

A GRAND TOTAL

The only goal I set for my one-year term as writer-in-residence on the Interisland ferry was to ride once or twice a week, studying and writing to create this essay collection. Although I didn't record the date of every ride, with the exception of a few weeks, I maintained that schedule throughout the year. When I finished my stint, I combed journals, blog posts, photographs, and my calendar to arrive at this tally I never could have imagined:

- 150-ish hours on the Interisland
- 30 journal entries
- 18 blog posts, August 2, 2018 to August 29, 2019, at www.writingtheinterisland.org
- 10 rough drafts of essays for this collection
- 1 essay, "Salish Sea Account," published in *For Love of Orcas*
- 12 others joining me throughout the year to write together aboard the ferry
- 0 whale sightings
- 100s of sightings of other marine life including harbor seals, bull kelp, cormorants, and gulls

- 1 rainbow
- 1 adult birthday celebration
- 1 Floating Ukelele Jam with 15 ukelele, banjolele, and guitar players
- 1 holiday get-together of mah-jong players
- 4 bouquets from a crew member's garden
- 1 ferry stranding on San Juan Island when the Lopez dock froze
- 5 jigsaw puzzles in progress at any given time on tables in the passenger cabin
- 50 or so cups of coffee consumed
- hundreds of photographs to jog my memory and post on my blog
- dozens of enlightening conversations with passengers and crew
- countless research articles, news stories, and books read
- several naps, my writer-in-residence table tent stashed away
- uncountable—the number of people who said, "That's so cool!" when I explained what I was doing.

The total of this adventure? Grand.

The
Salish Sea

The sea lives in every one of us.
—ROBERT WYLAND
artist and conservationist

PETITION FOR A NAME CHANGE

KING COUNTY DISTRICT COURT
WASHINGTON STATE

Date: 2008-2009

IN RE THE PETITION OF:

Current Name: Puget Sound, Northern Puget Sound

Applying for a court order which will change the current name to: The Salish Sea

The following statements are made under penalty of perjury.

1. Are you currently a resident of Washington? Yes.

And British Columbia, also. The Salish Sea's coastline is 4,642 miles, extending from the north end of the Strait of Georgia and Desolation Sound in British Columbia, through the Strait of Juan de Fuca and Puget Sound in the State of Washington. The Salish Sea includes 419 islands, a sea surface area of 6,535 square miles, and a maximum depth of 2,133 feet. Population of species living in the Salish Sea: 39 mammals (including approximately 8 million individual humans);172 birds; 253 fish; 2 reptiles; and more than 3,000 macro-invertebrates (visible without a microscope).

2. Have you had a name change prior to this petition? (Date, place, reason) Yes.

Captain George Vancouver renamed parts of these waters in 1792 after Lieutenant Peter Puget led an expedition off the current city of Seattle into southward waters. Most of the mapping and exploring was done by officers in small boats. Vancouver referred to the area, restricted to south of the Tacoma Narrows, as Puget Sound. Since that time, the area covered by the name Puget Sound "crept" northward with southern Georgia Strait and the area around the San Juan Islands known as "northern Puget Sound."

3. Name change requested for the following reason(s). (Please explain):

In the early 1970s, people began to worry about the negative effect of oil tankers from Alaska passing through the Strait of Juan de Fuca to refineries in the U.S. and Canada. In that era, an average of 24.5 large oil spills occurred annually worldwide. Some environmental scientists, like Bert Webber, believe using a single "brand" for all of Washington State's inland marine waters will encourage state residents to identify more strongly with the need for its protection. Webber and others also expect a new name will bring attention to the ecosystem interrelationships of the inland marine waters of both British Columbia and Washington State. Additionally, tribes around the inland sea share a historical connection with the Coast

Salish language. The name Salish Sea acknowledges the first peoples who live on the shores of this inland sea.

4. Is this name change petition made for any illegal or fraudulent purpose? No.

Virtually all of the Indigenous tribes around Puget Sound and the Strait of Georgia have links to the inland Salish and likely have a common origin. However, there is no single unifying name that the Indigenous people use for the Salish Sea ecosystem. They have their own descriptive terms for smaller parts of it, but the entire area has not been named. Since most of the Indigenous people in this region are of a Salish background, it seems appropriate to call this the Salish Sea.

Since 2000, tribal leaders from both British Columbia and Washington State have recognized the need to work together to protect and restore the health of this estuarine ecosystem, which has been damaged by the eight million people living around its perimeter. In 2005, seventy tribes and First Nations from Washington State and British Columbia collectively formed the "Coast Salish Gathering." The gathering's focus is to work with the governments of Canada and the United States to protect and manage the resources of the Salish Sea. Naming it bestows a sense of place that puts the area's natural resource issues in better perspective.

5. Will this name change be detrimental to the interests of anyone else? No.

This name change merely reflects the integrated ecosystem of the inland sea that shares mixed saltwater and freshwater as well as similar marine life.

We declare under penalty of perjury under the laws of the State of Washington that the foregoing statements in this petition are true and correct.

Petitioners:

Bert Webber, retired environmental and marine sciences professor,
Western Washington University
Coast Salish tribes of Washington State
First Nations People of Canada
George Harris, elder, Chemainus First Nation on Vancouver Island
Washington State Board of Geographic Names
United States Board of Geographic Names
Geographical Names Board of Canada
The Cabinet of the Province of British Columbia

POSTSCRIPT

This isn't how the name was changed (that was done over several years by the various name boards listed above as petitioners), but the form of a name change petition allows me to condense approximately twenty years of efforts into a brief essay.

Following the name change, the Coast Salish Peoples of Washington State and the First Nations of British Columbia celebrated in mid-July of 2010. They gathered at the Songhee First Nation in Esquimalt, BC. Over twenty-five hundred participants celebrated and formally recognized the Salish Sea name in word, dance, and song.

Still, only five percent of Washingtonians recognize the name, Salish Sea.

SALISH SEA ACCOUNT

Every single person counts. Just like every single emission counts. Every single kilo. Everything counts.

—GRETA THUNBERG

account—noun.
Report, story, log, tally, balance sheet, debt

2009, the year the U.S. Board on Geographic Names adopted the name Salish Sea to pay tribute to the first inhabitants of the region, the Coast Salish peoples.

7,000 square miles—the total marine area of the Salish Sea. These inland waters include Washington State's Puget Sound, the Strait of Juan de Fuca, the San Juan Islands, and the Strait of Georgia.

8,000,000 people live and work beside the Salish Sea.

73 Southern Resident killer whales (orcas) live in J, K, and L pods in the Salish Sea as of 2- 18-21, down from 86 when they were first listed as endangered in 2005.

30 Chinook/king salmon are typical in an orca's daily diet.

J-35 (also known as Tahlequah) is a 20-year-old orca whose newborn calf survived for only 30 minutes on 7-24-18.

17, the number of days Tahlequah carried the 400-pound body of her dead calf through the sea.

1,000 miles, the distance Tahlequah traveled the Salish Sea with her pod while pushing her dead calf.

17 minutes of silence observed at vigils following the death of Tahlequah's calf.

J-50 (also known as Scarlet), the latest Southern Resident to die on 9-13-18. The 3-year-old female began losing weight in 2017.

on account of—
owing to, due to, as a consequence of

3 main threats to Southern Residents: insufficient salmon, toxic water, noise pollution.

4 dams on the Lower Snake River impede Chinook salmon migration to breeding habitat.

130,000 adult salmon and steelhead returned to the Snake River to spawn in the 1950s; in 2017, there were less than 10,000.

3.6 billion dollars (U.S.) spent by the Canadian government to buy Kinder Morgan's Trans Mountain pipeline. The goal: to expand transport of low-grade tar sands oil from Alberta, Canada, to refineries in Northwest Washington.

7 times more oil tankers (each holding 25,000,000 gallons of tar sands oil mixed with volatile organic diluents, including benzene) will travel the Salish Sea if the Trans Mountain pipeline expands.

0 chance to clean up tar sands oil (diluted bitumen or "dil bit") and protect first responders and marine life from toxic chemicals when tankers spill.

96 commercial whale-watching boats operated in the Salish Sea in 2015, up from 63 in 1999.

$40,000,000–$55,000,000 was generated by the whale watching industry in 2015 (San Juan Tourism Bureau).

accountable—adjective.
Responsible, liable, comprehensible, understandable

1 Canadian Federal Court of Appeal overturned approval of the Trans Mountain oil pipeline expansion because the federal government failed to adequately consult First Nations.

44 state, tribal, provincial and federal officials served on Washington Governor Inslee's Southern Resident Orca Task Force. After two years of work, in 2019, the task force presented 49 recommendations that will lead to better water quality, a healthier ecosystem, and more robust salmon runs. They dedicated the final report to Tahlequah and to the two new orca calves born in 2019 (L124 and J56).

50 percent reduction in acoustic disturbance and a 15 percent increase in Chinook/king salmon would achieve the 2.3percent annual SRKW growth needed to assure survival.

Countless—the efforts to pay our overdue debt to Tahlequah, her calf, and the Salish Sea.

SO MUCH TO LEARN

Not everyone can claim to have a professional mermaid as a class-mate. You read right. Davina Liberty (formerly from California, now residing on Orcas Island) has received certification as a mermaid and uses her skill to teach others about ocean protection. In the summer of 2019, Davina and I were among twenty-eight participants from throughout the U.S. and Canada in the Whale Museum's Marine Naturalist Training Program. The group also included the son of an aquarium builder, retired nurses, a publisher, and a former emergency medicine physician. The training left me with my head spinning, my heart pounding, and my spirits low.

During the six-day training, I recognized just how much I didn't know about the Salish Sea and its endangered marine life. I was in the right place to learn more, though. The Whale Museum on San Juan Island has been training marine naturalists since 1994. Its intensive course includes in-depth presentations and observations of the ecology and conservation of local marine species by naturalists, environmental educators, and scientists.

I'm still processing my Dropbox full of PowerPoint presentations, a bulging three-ring binder, and my journal from the training. What I *do* know, though, is my awe and love for the Salish Sea is greater than ever after immersing myself in facts, images, and observations about life and beauty on the shores and in the water. Not just the beloved Southern Resident killer whales, but also the myriad marine mammals, invertebrates, birds, bugs, and plants that live in the Salish Sea. More than I had ever realized.

Yet, fears and deep grief live alongside the glory of the Salish Sea for me. Some days the celebration of the marine environment guides and inspires me. On others, sorrow and hopelessness dominate. On August 16, 2019, two weeks after I completed the training program, I had one of those despairing days when I learned the San Juan Island's Center for Whale Research reported three whale deaths. Joe Gaydos, Science Director of the Sea Doc Society, responded, "There is nothing good about losing three animals in a population that was numbered at 76. In no way can I find a silver lining to this news."

Another water-based location to study the Salish Sea—the University of Washington (UW) Friday Harbor Laboratories—is a short ferry ride from my home on Lopez Island to San Juan Island. Faculty and researchers from the university and around the world go there to study oceanography, chemistry, biology, ecology, and other marine disciplines.

In 1903, Friday Harbor was chosen by the UW for a marine biology field station because the waters around San Juan Island were relatively free from pollution. Most of the 490-acre tract of land on which Friday Harbor Laboratories is located is a biological preserve. "The Labs" also manage biological preserves on other islands so scientists and students can collect representatives of nearly all major groups of marine algae, invertebrates, and fish. The varied terrestrial and freshwater habitats also offer diverse flora and fauna. In honor of the Lab's seventieth anniversary, alumni founded the Whale Museum, the first museum in the country devoted to a species living in the wild.

Research at the Labs is conducted throughout the year, and faculty offer courses during autumn, spring, and summer. Various college-level groups visit for field trips, meetings, and symposia. Resembling a child's fantasy of summer camp, the preserve's laboratories, library, cabins, cafeteria, and research vessel draw students and teachers here from around the world.

One facility that particularly interested me was the Whiteley Center. Funded by the Helen R. Whiteley Foundation, the center offers lodging, study space, and access to its library for scholarly work and creative activity by people in all disciplines. I applied for a two-and-a-half-week residency seeking solitude, quiet, and an inspiring seaside setting to continue work on the essays in this collection. At the end of January 2020, I arrived with boxes of books and journals and received a key to "Charlie's Cottage," a one-bedroom cabin looking onto the harbor, a protected bay, and moss-carpeted boulders.

The cottage offered everything I needed to prepare meals, rest, and roll out my yoga mat. Many nights I ate dinner by candlelight and the fireplace glow. Charlie's Cottage is named after a former graduate student, Charles Lambert, known for his "enthusiasm, expertise, persistence, and devotion to his science." Charlie's bio explains he and his wife "came to UW with a passion for tunicates." You bet I had to look that up to discover tunicates are invertebrates, commonly called sea squirts. Charlie studied the local version, *Ascidia callosum*.

The Whiteley Center's main building houses three study rooms, furnished with two desks, an easy chair, bookshelves, and a stone fireplace. Each study is named for a friend of the Labs, and I was offered "Bob's Study" for my work space. A brief biography under his photo explains Bob had a passion for marine invertebrates, developed many advanced courses, and eventually served as the Friday Harbor Labs director. "Bob was our leader," the bio concludes.

After I unloaded books and journals into Bob's Study, I saw a woman in the hallway. She smiled and asked, "Are you one of the scholars?"

I hesitated. "Scholar" isn't a word I tend to use to describe myself. But that's the term the Whiteley Center applies to those they accept for residencies.

My study desk sat in front of a window looking across Friday Harbor toward the marina, the ferry landing, and the town. From another window, Madrones on a mossy bluff reached toward the bay. The gas fireplace warmed and brightened the room on gray days (many of them during my tenure). When I arrived to work, I exchanged my rubber boots for wool slippers and turned on my desk lamp. My laptop, books, journals, a thermos of tea, a mug, a candle, and a palm-sized ceramic heart sat on the desktop. Notably absent were piles of unfiled papers, stacks of mail, and other distractions found at home.

I was at my desk every morning as the MV *Tillikum*—the ferry I rode and wrote on during my tenure as Writer-in-Residence on the Interisland—snugged into its berth at the dock. I reviewed the blue binder from the Marine Naturalist Training Program and journal entries from my time as Writer-in-Residence, read prose and poetry about the Salish Sea, and searched online sources about whales.

Another scholar shared my study room for a few days, and we swapped news about a new viral outbreak in China. We talked of hoping the virus, COVID-19, wouldn't make its way to the U.S. However, within a few weeks after I left the Whiteley Center, the first cases appeared in this country, with a large number of them attributed to a nursing home less than one hundred miles from the islands.

As I write in January 2021, studying *on* the Salish Sea as I did last year remains limited. Ferry passengers are advised to avoid the vessels' indoor cabins, the ferry system's Writer-in-Residence program has been put on hold, and the Marine Naturalist Training Program is currently offered on-line only. The Whiteley Center still hosts scholars who follow COVID protocols.

The world has been through numerous peaks and valleys in cases, millions of deaths, and a wobbly introduction of the COVID vaccine. The threat of COVID-19 is dire, but we're fairly confident of its passing. The Salish Sea and its inhabitants, however, remain in peril, demanding we continue to learn.

A PLACE THE SUN
NEVER REACHES

The opening of an "On Being" podcast made me stop mid-step. I'd selected an episode on my mobile phone to drown out traffic noise while walking in the city. Host Krista Tippett began,

"Oceanographer Sylvia Earle was the first person to walk solo on the bottom of the sea, under a quarter mile of water." Earle made history off the coast of Oahu, Hawaii in 1979 at age forty-four. It was the deepest dive ever done without a tether to the surface, a record Earle still holds. The feat earned her the title "Her Deepness."

Walk on the bottom of the sea? Sylvia Earle? I'd never heard of her, but I soon discovered I needed to know more about this marine biologist and botanist, *National Geographic* explorer-in-residence, and former chief scientist of the National Oceanic and Atmospheric Administration.

These probably aren't titles Sylvia Earle ever imagined for herself as a child, even though she was "a critter person." Earle spent part of her childhood on New Jersey farmland until her family moved near the ocean in Clearwater, Florida. She told Tippett she attributes her interest in animals to her mother, who usually had "a hospital for small, injured animals...And they mostly recovered...."

In a *New Yorker* profile ten years after her walk, Earle spoke about the impact of being one of the first marine scientists to use scuba equipment to explore the ocean. The walk, she says, "caused me to think very hard about how I could convey something about the animals and plants in the ocean—the system which actually dominates our planet. Now we have been able to see, first of all, that the ocean is alive. When you pick up any piece of this planet, you find that, one way or another, it's attached to everything else—if you jiggle over here, something is going to wiggle over there."

Much of the ocean is dark, all the time, and Earle, now in her eighties, has spent thousands of hours over the past sixty years in places the sun never reaches. She explained to Tippett: "Well, the first experience is going through the sunlit area and into what generally is known as the 'twilight zone,' where sunlight fades, and darkness begins to take over. You can see shapes, but not really distinct forms." Around six hundred feet, Earle says, "... it's really, really dark. A thousand feet and below, it is truly dark."

In 2011 during remarks when she received the Royal Geographical Society's Patrons Medal, she estimated only about five percent of the ocean had even been seen, let alone explored. This new frontier, she said, "is in trouble, and that means we're in trouble."

Earle told Tippett that saving the ocean is her life. "There are policies put in place in the 1950s, '60s, and '70s, and even current policies, that seem, perversely, to be based on the assumption that there's a large quantity of excess out there that we can extract from the ocean, in terms of the number of fish or whales."

In the *New Yorker* profile, Earle was even more graphic.

"We're ripping through our resources at an alarming rate, consuming and not giving back, chewing up forests for lumber and newsprint and not sustaining those forests, using freshwater resources without sustaining our rivers and lakes, wreaking havoc on our coastlines and the entire ocean system. And it has been estimated that we are losing ten thousand species a year—plants, insects, birds, fish, mammals, microorganisms—many of them before we even know they exist."

In July 2018, the death of a newborn orca held the world's attention as, for seventeen days and one thousand miles, the calf's mother, Tahlequah, carried her dead baby on her forehead. That drama convinced large numbers of people that the Salish Sea is in trouble. The "ripping through our resources ...consuming and not giving back" Earle describes has diminished food supplies—Chinook salmon in particular—for the Southern Resident killer whales, shortening their lives and making reproduction and survival more tenuous. Oil tankers and other water vessels, including whale watching boats and ferries, create an underwater din that interferes with sounds whales need for communication and echolocation. Toxicants from oil spills, chemical contaminants, and plastics foul the water and food so vital to these sea mammals.

"There is a terribly terrestrial mindset about what we need to do to take care of the planet," Earle believes, "as if the ocean somehow doesn't matter or is so big, so vast that it can take care of itself, or that there is nothing that we could possibly do that we could harm the ocean." Those attitudes about the sea have contributed to humans' actions for decades. "We have gone from one species after another and drawn them down by as much as 90 percent. In some cases, 99 percent of some species are gone because of our capacity to find, kill, extract, and market, consume, things such as—well, we already, by the 1950s, had demonstrated our power to do this with whales."

Earle wishes everybody could go live underwater, if only for a day. "We need this sense of the continuing interconnectedness of the system as part of the common knowledge," she says, "so that politicians feel it and believe it, and so that voters feel it and believe it, and so that kids feel it and believe it so that they'll grow up with an ethic.

Because what we do—or don't do—now will be an inheritance for all time."

I'll never dive to the depths Sylvia Earle has. But the longer I reside on the Salish Sea, inhale its briny scent, and watch and hear its tides ebb and flow, the more interconnected I feel to this suffering ecosystem. I can't spend a day underwater, let alone take you with me, but maybe my words can compel us all to do whatever we can to save the sea, including the place the sun never reaches.

THE BLISTER OF GREED

We're ripping through our resources at an alarming rate,
consuming and not giving back ... wreaking havoc on our
coastlines and the entire ocean system.

—SYLVIA EARLE
oceanographer and marine biologist

Rain slickens the ferry's deck,
spatters droplets on my glasses
soon fogged
by the passenger cabin's warmth.

My shoulders
hunch over my laptop's keys,
and my fingers tap
as the ferry crosses
from one island to another.

The vessel drags my fears
for the Salish Sea
in its wake.

Thundering echoes of tankers
and tour boats
bleed into whale conversations,
muffle the timbre of wisdom
an orca cow sings
to her calf.

The grasp for more,
more—money, power, self-interest—
gnaws the fragile balance
among puffins and porpoises,
sea stars and sea urchins,
bull kelp and blue herons,
between marine life and human life.

The sea notices,
surrounds the blister of greed,
drenching it in the sting
of salt.

VOWS FOR THE SALISH SEA

In 1979, just shy of a decade after the first Earth Day celebration, I stood beside a young man with brown hair and a beard with red glints. I wore a flower-print peasant dress and sandals. He wore tan, corduroy slacks, Birkenstock sandals, and a cotton tunic he bought on a college trip to Greece. A minister reminded us how to keep our commitment alive: grow; change; maintain the capacity for wonder, spontaneity, and humor; remain flexible, warm, and sensitive; give fully to each other and show your real feelings to one another; save time for each other, no matter what demands were made upon your day; nurture each other to fullness and wholeness.

My groom and I were twenty-six. At that tender age, we couldn't fully understand the challenges of honoring those vows. We didn't know the ways we would change as individuals and as a couple. We couldn't imagine the forces outside of us that would test our agreement to maintain wonder, flexibility, and honesty.

Every so often, I open the dust-covered photo album from our wedding day and re-read the vows. Sometimes my husband Jerry and I say them out loud again to each other. They remind me of my responsibility to keep my commitment alive.

Soon after I ended my term as Writer-in-Residence on the Interisland ferry, Jerry and I marked the fortieth anniversary of our marriage. Vows were on my mind, both for us as a couple and as protectors of the Salish Sea.

As the air, the land, the sea, and many of their creatures suffer, I'm deeply aware of my responsibility to help keep them healthy. I rely on them for wonder, beauty, nurture, and presence. I used to think the natural environment didn't ask much of me in exchange for its gifts. But now, after learning just how close Southern Resident orcas are to extinction as a result of our actions, I'm ready to commit.

Marriage vows typically list what two people promise they WILL do, and I support that positive approach. But at this time of climate chaos, perhaps it's equally important to promise to NOT participate in actions that harm the earth. There are many actions we must cease. Thus, my vows for the Salish Sea.

> I WILL watch the Salish Sea and the life she supports with reverence and wonder.
> I WILL NOT observe the sea from a whale-watching boat.
> I WILL honor the name, Salish Sea, given to her in 2009 to acknowledge her geography and history.
> I WILL NOT speak names that deny the presence of Indigenous communities.
> I WILL seek out and amplify the messages of Black, Indigenous, and People of Color activists and environmental leaders.
> I WILL NOT ignore the intersections of environmentalism and social justice.
> I WILL continue to study the effects of climate change and human behavior on the health of the Salish Sea.
> I WILL NOT use toxins like moss killers, pesticides, or fertilizers on my lawn or driveway; they end up in storm water that empties into the sea and then into the marine food chain. As the toxins move up the food chain, they become more concentrated; orcas consume them and store them in their fat reserves. Female orcas pass the contaminants to their babies through breast milk.
> I WILL keep my car in good condition so oil and brake fluid don't contaminate storm water.

I WILL NOT dump chemical or pharmaceutical waste in the sewer/septic system; like pesticides, they end up in marine life systems and eventually in orca blubber.

I WILL grieve what we stand to lose and what we've already lost.

I WILL NOT avoid the bad news about the perils the Southern Resident whales face, nor accept they're inevitable.

I WILL continue to study more about salmon habitat and protection.

I WILL NOT eat Chinook/king salmon. This breed is the best source of nutrition for Southern Residents. Since 1984, the Chinook salmon population has decreased sixty percent.

I WILL speak honestly with my community and my elected officials about personal and collective actions that endanger the Salish Sea.

I WILL NOT take for granted my inhalations spiced with salt; Great Blue Herons squawking at my intrusion; river otters scampering across rocky beaches; the undersea forest of kelp washed up on beaches after a storm; and orcas swishing their tails to balance upright and spy on me.

———

The groom's brown hair and red-tinged beard have turned gray. I now wear sweaters and jeans instead of peasant dresses. Much has changed in our lives since 1979—degrees, jobs, children, a grandchild, moves, deaths of parents and siblings. Yet, we take our vows as seriously as the day we first spoke them to each other.

I'm taking my commitments to the Salish Sea seriously, too. Here's one more.

I WILL speak up. The lives of my son and daughters, my granddaughter, and the sons and daughters and grandchildren of our beloved native whales depend on all of us raising our voices. What would your commitment to *your* environment look like? Will you join me in making one?

The
Orcas
(Southern Resident killer whales)

We still talk in terms of conquest. We still haven't become mature enough to think of ourselves as only a tiny part of a vast and incredible universe. Man's attitude toward nature is today critically important simply because we have now acquired a fateful power to alter and destroy nature.

—RACHEL CARSON

O IS FOR ORCA

An Alphabetical Excursion through Orca Whale Characteristics

A is for age. Male orcas (bulls) tend to live into their forties, but sometimes up to fifty years. Females (cows) typically live into their eighties. Granny, venerable matriarch of J pod, is estimated to have lived to one hundred. Cows reach reproductive maturity between the ages of thirteen and fifteen. Bulls begin breeding around twenty-five years of age. Calves are weaned after they reach one year.

B is for breathing. Unlike humans, killer whales are voluntary breathers—they have to consciously remember to take a breath every time they need air. They breathe through a blowhole on the top of their heads, similar to the nostril in other mammals. When closed, the blowhole is completely airtight; to take a breath, muscles contract to open the blowhole's flap.

This means orcas can't sleep the same way humans do, or they would drown. Marine biologists believe orcas sleep by shutting down one hemisphere of the brain at a time, allowing them to rest while still maintaining their voluntary breathing.

B is also for brain. Killer whales have the second-largest brain of any animal. A mature orca whale brain weighs between twelve and fifteen pounds; the only animal with a larger brain (around eighteen pounds) is the sperm whale. The average human brain weighs nine pounds.

C is for Chinook salmon, the red and silver-toned fish that makes up about eighty percent of the Southern Resident orca diet. Chinook salmon (also known as kings) are the largest and fattiest of all the Pacific salmon, thus are a good source of calories for the extremely active Southern Residents. They hatch in freshwater streams, then make their way hundreds of miles to the ocean to enrich their bodies with carbon and nitrogen. Chinooks (as well as other species of salmon) spend years in the ocean before finding their way back to the rivers where they were born to mate, lay eggs, and die. The nutrients their bodies carry back upriver become important food and fertilizer for land and river ecosystems, helping everything from trees to birds to bears. Chinooks are shrinking in size and number, however. In the early 1900s, they typically weighed sixty to seventy pounds and sometimes as much as one hundred pounds; today, their average weight is around thirty pounds.

D is for dams. Wild Pacific salmon spend most of their lives in the Pacific Ocean, but freshwater rivers and streams are where their lives begin and end. The Columbia River Basin in the Pacific Northwest was once among the greatest salmon-producing river systems in the world, likely responsible for over half the Chinook salmon in the range of Southern Resident orcas. In the 1960s, the Government built four hydroelectric dams on the lower Snake River in Washington—Ice Harbor, Little Goose, Lower Monumental, and Lower Granite. They block more than half of salmon spawning and rearing habitat access. Many people believe the dwindling source of orca nutrition is due to dams on rivers. In 2000, the Government acknowledged that removing these dams would help recover endangered salmon and whales. But in July 2020, the Trump administration announced the Lower Snake dams will not be removed.

Previous dam removals around the country have been successful at aiding fish recovery and river restoration. In fact, Western Washington saw the largest dam removal thus far in the country with the demolition of two dams on the Elwha River in 2011 and 2014. The project opened seventy miles of habitat that had been blocked for a century. Scientists are seeing all five species of salmon native to the river, including Chinook, coming back.

E is for echolocation, the sixth sense of orcas. They use echolocation to talk to each other and hunt. Orcas produce clicks, whistles, and pulsed calls that are transmitted by a fatty tissue called melon. This produces a directional and amplified sound that travels in water up to 800 meters. The lower jaw receives the wave which travels through the auditory nerve to the brain.

Through this sense, orcas not only see the shape of the object, they can also see inside it. Like a submarine using sonar, or an obstetrician with a sonogram, orcas are able to send out pulses of sound that will send back information used to create a visual picture. This sophisticated technique is able to detect the difference between species of salmon, so they can expend their energy into catching the fattest and largest salmon, Chinook. Each pod possesses unique calls that are learned and culturally transmitted among individuals. These calls maintain group cohesion and serve as family badges.

E is also for Echo (J42), a female whale born in May 2007. She spent lots of time babysitting her little sister, J50 (Scarlet), the first orca to receive medical treatment in the wild.

F is for fin. Whales generally have four fins: two pectoral fins (instead of arms), a caudal fin (also called the tail), and a dorsal fin. The pectoral fins, just behind the head, are paddle-shaped and are used for steering, turning, and stopping. They serve as the whales' rudders and stabilizers. A network of nerves inside the pectoral fins helps regulate body temperature. The caudal fin is used for propulsion of the whale, with up-and-down movements created by powerful muscles. Male orcas have the largest dorsal fin (up to six feet tall) of any marine mammal. In females, the dorsal fin is a bit shorter and more curved. It acts like the keel of a boat, keeping the whale from rolling side to side while swimming.

G is for Granny (J2). Believed to be the world's longest-living Southern Resident orca. Estimated birth year, 1911; Granny died in 2016. Many people thought of her as the symbol of the matriarchy defining the social structure of killer whales.

H is for health. The health of Southern Residents is threatened by multiple causes. Dwindling supplies of Chinook salmon lead to emaciation. A peanut shape to a whale's head suggests life-threatening weight loss.

H is also for heartbreaking. With every death of a Southern Resident, people worry that the species will become extinct.

I is for identify. Sparked by the increase in live capture for aquaria and public concern, scientists have been studying resident pods along the northern Pacific coast of the United States and Canada since 1970. By 1973, photographs were being used to identify individuals based on differences in saddle color pattern, dorsal fin shapes, and other identifying marks and scars. Identified orcas have all been numbered, and careful records are kept of their re-sightings.

J is for J pod, K is for K pod, L is for L pod. The Southern Resident killer whale community is formed of three pods (groups) known as J, K and L. Orcas generally live in pods consisting of several females, calves, several males, and/or juveniles. Some pods consist of a mother and her offspring who stay with her for life. This type of matrilineal family structure has been observed in the Pacific Northwest, where resident pods have been documented as stable, consistent matriarchal family groups with several generations traveling together. Each pod has its own dialect, but they also share a set of calls so that when they come together, they can communicate, socialize, and mate.

According to orcanetwork.org, as of February 17, 2021, J pod had twenty-four members, K pod had seventeen, and L pod had thirty-four. If you include Lolita/Tokitae, the L pod orca in captivity at the Miami Seaquarium, the total number of Southern Residents was seventy-six.

The pod letters were first assigned to the two communities of fish-eating killer whales in the 1970s and were based on observed family relationships and association between the families and their unique dialects and vocalizations. The letters from A to I were used for the larger Northern Resident community, whose range is from Alaska to the north of Vancouver Island, Canada.

The Center for Whale Research has documented these families since 1976. The Center gives each newborn Southern Resident calf that survives the first day a unique identification. The letter J, K, or L denotes the pod of the mother's family, and the calf will stay with her family for life. The number is the next available. For example, the latest calf born to J pod in 2020 was J58, and the next calf born to a J pod mother will be J59.

While researchers love numbers, non-scientists love names. So, the Whale Museum asks its members to vote for a name for new calves of the year. Usually, the calf name will have some association with the mother. For example, the son of Eclipse was named Nova, to keep the celestial theme.

M is for mammal. Orca whales live in the ocean, but they're not fish. They are mammals.

And M is for Mike (J26), older brother of Echo and Scarlet. Mike was named in honor of Mike Bigg, known as the father of killer whale research. He was the first person to realize that killer whales have unique saddle patches and fins that, like a fingerprint, make it possible to identify every animal over its lifetime.

N is for noise. Female orcas are most thrown off from foraging when boats and vessels intrude closer than four hundred yards. Male and female orcas alike change their behavior when vessels come close — females more than males. Females will either stop foraging if they are, or not initiate foraging dives. Males are more typically seen in deeper water, foraging alone. The complex maneuvers orcas undertake to successfully hunt prey involve reconnaissance at the surface, exploration, then the actual deep, foraging dive to nail a fleeing salmon, all using echolocation to "see" in the dark depths. It's like being at a noisy party and having to keep raising your voice; it's exhausting.

O is for orca. The first half of the killer whale's scientific name— *Orcinus orca*—comes from the Latin for "of the realms of the dead." It's commonly known as the Killer whale. However, the orca isn't actually a whale; it's the largest member of the dolphin, or toothed whale, family. Orcas live in every ocean of the world. Part of the suborder of mammals called toothed whales, they have ten to thirteen conical teeth in each jaw that interlock to crush and shred their prey. Orcas swim about seventy-five miles per day, traveling eight miles per hour on average; however, they can burst through the water at thirty miles per hour when they choose. Each black and white orca has a unique gray saddle-shaped patch on its back, enabling researchers to identify them individually.

Orcas, with a capital O, is for an island in the Salish Sea. It's NOT named for the orca whales. Rather, it's a shortened form of the name "Horcasitas," part of the full name of Juan Vicente de Güemes

Padilla Horcasitas y Aguayo, the Viceroy of Mexico. Horcasitas sent an expedition led by Spanish explorer Francisco de Eliza to the Pacific Northwest in 1791.

P is for pod. Killer whales are highly social, and most live in social groups called pods (groups of related individuals seen together more than half the time). Individual whales tend to stay in their original pods. Pods typically consist of a few to twenty or more animals, and larger groups sometimes form for temporary social interactions, mating, or seasonal concentrations of prey. The pods have intensely strong family bonds, staying together through the generations for life. They share food, sleep together, play, hunt, explore and travel as a group.

P is also for Princess Angeline (J17), a female born in 1977 and declared missing in 2019. She was named in honor of the daughter of Chief Sealth (Seathl), anglicized to Seattle, a Duwamish elder after whom Seattle is named. Princess Angeline was the mother of Tahlequah (J35).

Q is for questions. We still have many questions about how to return the Southern Resident orca population, so these animals are no longer endangered. Perhaps the most important question is, "How can I help?"

R is for resident. In the Pacific Northwest, the group of killer whales that feed exclusively on salmon, ideally Chinook/king salmon, are referred to as residents. They're not to be confused with the first writer-in-residence with the Washington State ferry system, even though she also eats salmon (but not Chinook). Transient whales feed only on marine mammals. See **S is for Southern Resident killer whales** and **T is for transients**.

S is for Southern Resident killer whales. The fish eaters, or Southern Residents, in the North Pacific, eat mostly salmon and tend to prefer Chinook salmon, likely because it is the biggest and fattest of the salmon species. In the early 1970s, two separate and distinct populations of fish-eating resident killer whales were found in the Pacific Northwest. These two communities were designated the Southern community and the Northern community, in direct relation to their travel patterns in and around the waters of Vancouver Island. The Southern community of orcas was most often encountered off the southern end of Vancouver Island, including the inland marine waters of Washington State. The Northern community was most often encountered in the northern Vancouver Island region, including Queen Charlotte Sound and southern Southeast Alaska. The annual spring-through-summer feeding grounds for the Southern Resident killer whales encompass the inland marine waters (the Salish Sea) of Washington State, particularly around the San Juan Islands and southwestern British Columbia. In winter, they follow food along the outer coast, from as far north as Haida Gwaii in British Columbia to as far south as California's Monterrey Bay.

T is for transients. Also called Bigg's killer whales, transients eat other marine mammals, such as seals, sea lions, porpoises and minke whales. This requires different hunting techniques, and thus, a different language. There's no evidence that transients and residents can communicate with each other.

T is also for taxonomy. According to the Integrated Taxonomic Information System (ITIS), the taxonomy of orcas is:
  Kingdom · Animalia
  Phylum · Chordata
  Class · Mammalia
  Order · Cetacea
  Family · Delphinidae
  Genus & species · *Orcinus orca*

U is for underwater. Killer whales rely on underwater sound to feed, communicate, and navigate. Noise from ocean vessels can interfere with the sounds whales rely on.

V is for vision. The orca's eyes are located just below and in front of the eyespot. Broadly speaking, whales see details about ten times worse than humans and several times worse than your dog or cat. Unlike nocturnal rodents or humans, whales see the world in monochrome, only in shades of gray. The water we see as blue, they see as black. The lens has to do everything in the whale eye; it's circular, instead of flattish like lenses of humans, in order to provide sufficient focus. The cetacean pupil closes like a smiling mouth.

Whale eyes are located on each side of the head, so they don't have binocular vision. In order to safeguard their eyeballs, there are glands at the outer corneal layer and eyelids, which secrete a substance that lubricates and flushes the eye of any impurities.

While humans tread water, whales spy-hop. With their pectoral fins, they position themselves vertically above the water-line, then poke their heads out of the water in a slow, controlled manner. They sometimes stay in this position for minutes at a time to see what's happening at the surface.

W is for Whale Wise. Boat owners approaching too quickly, getting too close, or making too much noise can disrupt orcas, keeping them from finding food, socializing, resting, and other activities. The Be Whale Wise campaign started in the late 1990s to help protect orcas from these disturbances.

Initially, a partnership of governmental agencies, non-profits, and other stakeholders in the Salish Sea researched best vessel practices to protect the unique and fragile marine resources in the area. Today, the Be Whale Wise team helps create consistent messaging and education to commercial and private boaters on-shore, then reinforces the message on-the-water.

U.S. regulations require vessels to stay at least three hundred yards away on either side of a Southern Resident killer whale's path and four hundred yards out of the path, in front and behind the orcas.

W is also for weight. Orca calves weigh around four hundred pounds at birth. When they're mature, they can weigh up to six tons.

X is for OnyX (L87), a male born in 1992. He's believed to be the younger brother (by twenty years) of Spirit. When Onyx's mother died in 2005, he traveled with K Pod until 2010. Then, he began to travel with J8 (Speiden) and J2 (Granny). Even though both Speiden and Granny have died, Onyx remains with J Pod.

Y is for Yoda (K36), a female born in 1993.

Z is for zzzzz—sleeping. Because orcas are voluntary breathers (see **B is for breathing**), they can't sleep the same way humans do, or they would drown. They sleep by shutting down one hemisphere of their brain at a time, and they keep the eye on the "asleep" side of the brain open. Periodically, they alternate which side of the brain is sleeping, allowing them to rest while still maintaining their voluntary breathing.

CAN YOU HEAR ME?

I. HUMANS TO HUMANS

Can you hear me?
Here in Washington's San Juan Islands, locals and visitors alike often shout this question just before realizing their mobile phone call has been dropped.

You're muted.
Remember Zoom, FaceTime, and conference calls, those tools nearly everyone started using as COVID-19 drove us apart? A slash line through a red microphone icon signals our voices are silent to others, but we often don't notice until someone else on the call says, "We can't hear you. You're muted."

Where are you?
Our disembodied voices could be coming from almost anywhere now.

II. ORCA WHALES TO ORCA WHALES

Can you hear me?
I'm calling you through my melon, hoping you'll hear my clicks, buzzes, and whistles. I'm trying to alert you that big, fatty Chinook salmon are all around me. How do I know that? I forced breath through air sacs in my nose, creating sound waves; echoes bounced off the salmon in my path, passed through my lower jaw, vibrated my inner ear bones, and sent the message to my brain. You know, pretty much the same way Grandmother Whale explained that a bat uses sonar in the dark of night. I'd really like all of you to join me here for a salmon feast. Plus, I could use some help. It takes a lot of energy to catch even one of these delicious fish.

You're Muted
Or maybe it's that I can't hear you over the noises echoing in the straits, even when you raise your voices to be heard. Ferries, oil tankers, container ships, recreational boats, and whale-watch tours are in the same sonic zone we use to hunt and communicate.

Where are you?
Now I can't hear you—or those Chinooks. Sounds like you're near a cargo ship. That's the fifth one to come through while I've been hunting—just an average day in the Salish Sea. And it's going to get worse if that Canadian pipeline expands and increases oil tanker traffic seven-fold. Darn, I can't figure out where you are. Come here, come here! I need you. And where have the salmon disappeared to?

BEREAVEMENT

On July 24, 2018, an orca whale, known as Tahlequah, gave birth to a calf in the Salish Sea. Thirty minutes later, the newborn died. Tahlequah made headlines for days as she carried her dead calf on her head. Photographs and video footage documented Tahlequah's behavior, as well as that of her relatives who occasionally helped her carry her baby. It's likely they also helped feed her during her mourning.

Each day, I checked for news of Tahlequah's journey. She's one of seventy-four endangered Southern Resident killer whales (orcas) that live in the Salish Sea. I live on an island surrounded by that sea. Here, and all around the world, people mourned the calf's death and feared for Tahlequah's life.

On November 22, 1963, President John F. Kennedy was assassinated by a sniper's bullet as he and his wife, Jacqueline, waved from an open convertible to people along a parade route in Dallas, Texas. It was her first public appearance since the death of their baby, Patrick, three months earlier. She wore her blood-spattered, pink suit jacket and skirt throughout the rest of the day and at the swearing-in ceremony for Vice-President Lyndon Johnson aboard Air Force One.

I learned the news of Kennedy's assassination during P.E. class; I was in sixth grade. I sat on the gym floor and cried for my president. A friend asked, "What about Jackie?" For three days, the drapes in our living room were closed. All weekend, and through Monday, Mom, Dad, and I stepped away from the television only to go to the bathroom or to make something to eat. We sat in the living room together, ate dinner there, and watched until sign-off.

Tahlequah's behavior wasn't unusual. Orcas and other mammals, including gorillas, often carry their deceased young in what scientists widely understand to be an expression of grief.

For seventeen days, Tahlequah determinedly clung to her calf's pale, pink body, diving deeply to retrieve her each time she slid from her head. After covering a thousand miles, Tahlequah dropped the calf and rejoined the rest of her pod. Orca mothers typically carry their calves for a few hours or days. They know bereavement has its own timing. Scientists reported Tahlequah's witness was extraordinary in its duration—among documented examples, unprecedented. I think I would have done the same, not wanting to let go of my baby until I was washed in salty tears.

President Johnson's first proclamation declared Monday, November 25, a national day of mourning. On that day, President Kennedy's flag-draped casket left the Capitol rotunda on a caisson drawn by six gray horses, accompanied by one riderless black horse. At Mrs. Kennedy's request, the ceremony was modeled after the funeral of another assassinated president, Abraham Lincoln. Crowds lined

Pennsylvania Avenue as the caisson passed on its way to St. Matthew's Catholic Cathedral for a requiem Mass. Bystanders wept openly. During the twenty-one hours the president's body lay in state in the Capitol Rotunda, 250,000 people filed past the casket to pay their respects.

Mom, Dad, and I spent that national day of mourning watching it all, in living color, on our television. Jacqueline Kennedy's behavior was not unusual for a woman, a First Lady, in 1963. Her face wore little expression, no tears, no smile. Though I do remember a white handkerchief always present in her hand. As the flag-draped coffin passed the First Lady and her children, John Jr., who turned three that day, saluted. President Kennedy was buried with full military honors in Arlington Cemetery, where Jackie lit an eternal flame to forever mark the grave.

≈

A month after Tahlequah's calf's death, I joined 150 of my island neighbors on the shoreline for a wake. The sun shone that late August day, but a breeze chilled the air. A Swinomish tribal elder sang a lament to his drumbeat's rhythm as saltwater advanced and receded. A friend swirled a wooden mallet in a bronze singing bowl, signaling the beginning and end of seventeen minutes of silence.

The welfare of our children, grandchildren, and future generations is dependent upon caring for the Salish Sea and all its inhabitants. Are the bonds between humans and wildlife strong enough for us to stand for the orcas? We must recognize no amount of bereavement can erase the loss of an entire species.

TENACIOUS SCARLET

Female orca J50 received the name Scarlet for the rake marks seen on her body shortly after her birth in December 2014. Biologists believe the scars were signs of a difficult birth, with midwifing members of her pod pulling her out of her mother, J16 (Slick), with their teeth. As she grew, Scarlet captured people's hearts with her love for breaching, or leaping, in the water. Dr. Deborah Giles, research biologist at the University of Washington Center for Conservation Biology and the science and research director at the nonprofit Wild Orca, believes exuberance for life was Scarlet's trademark. Calling her "a damn spunky whale," Giles recalled Scarlet was once seen breaching forty times in a row, flinging herself out of the water with her body in an arc.

In 2018, Scarlet's spunkiness began to fade, and she became known widely for another reason. Always small, Scarlet began to show increasing signs of weight loss; she became so emaciated she had trouble swimming and holding her head up. Several biologists noted her breath smelled foul. All these signs indicated Scarlet was sick.

Biologists and veterinarians had been meeting and training for two years prior to Scarlet's decline to prepare for medical intervention for free-ranging killer whales, should the need arise. With only twenty-four breeding females in the Southern Resident whale population (as of February 2021), Scarlet's failing health raised concerns. If she didn't survive to child-bearing years, the orca community's growth could be even more significantly reduced. After numerous phone calls and meetings, the scientists agreed to a first-ever attempt to intervene.

According to Joe Gaydos, research director and veterinarian with the Orcas Island-based SeaDoc Society (a program of the University of California, Davis), top experts from governments, tribes, academia, the private sector, and non-profits stepped up to help Scarlet. They even consulted with SeaDoc's sister program, Gorilla Doctors. For over two decades, the program has provided health care for endangered mountain gorillas in central Africa. Gaydos said Gorilla Doctors' extreme veterinary involvement has helped with a four percent growth increase for these endangered animals. However, everyone working to help Scarlet never lost sight of the bigger picture, Gaydos said—recovery of the entire Southern Resident population by increasing salmon, decreasing underwater noise, and reducing human-made contaminants.

The emergency response was authorized under a Marine Mammal Protection Act permit issued by the National Oceanic and Atmospheric Administration. The permit required protecting Scarlet and the rest of J Pod, coordinating vessel traffic around the whales, and managing the amount of time vessels would spend near the pod.

Veterinarians have limited ability to remotely diagnose and treat disease in free-swimming orcas, and it's frustrating for them to work amid so much uncertainty. "Without a blood sample, for instance, it's hard to know exactly what's ailing the whale," Gaydos said. Despite their best efforts using Scarlet's history, visual and behavioral assessments, and evaluating her blow (breath) and fecal samples, they couldn't identify the cause of her symptoms. The best they could do was focus on treating potential secondary infections such as bacterial pneumonia and parasite infestation. Meanwhile, Scarlet continued to lose weight.

Throughout the year, Giles was shocked and dismayed at the changes in Scarlet. "You look at her, and you think, 'How can you even swim? You have no fat.'" Still, Giles maintained hope. "She is this tenacious animal, with this strong will to live. If any animal could make it through with a little extra support, it would be this animal."

One of the few experts in the region permitted to drive a boat amid the whales, Giles transported veterinarian Martin Haulena the day he was set to deliver a thirty-centimeter-long dart loaded with antibiotics. Scarlet swam nestled among her family members. "It took one hundred percent attention from everyone on the boat to follow the whales' every motion, moving like a member of the pod," Giles told *Seattle Times* reporter, Lynda V. Mapes, for her story published September 8, 2018. "It was a tricky shot, " Haulena told Mapes, "kneeling in the bow of a moving boat, in pursuit of a moving and fragile target."

I can't imagine trying to inject an animal under these conditions. Throughout my nursing career, I gave thousands of shots to humans, but the patient and I were always on land, and I used a syringe instead of a dart. The patient usually wasn't moving either, except for toddlers I immunized.

If Haulena's shot went in too hard, the needle-tipped dart could embed in Scarlet's flesh, doing more harm than good. Too soft, and the dart wouldn't fly accurately. If Haulena missed, he could hit Scarlet's dorsal fin, a dead-end for the medicine. And a shot to an eye or her belly would be devastating, possibly life-threatening.

Haulena told Mapes he'd darted plenty of entangled sea lions to anesthetize them so he could disentangle them from debris. But injecting a wild, moving killer whale was a first for the Vancouver Aquarium's head veterinarian.

Mapes watched a video of the intervention captured on Haulena's GoPro and reported, "With a thwack, the needle sailed from Haulena's rifle and stuck, right where he wanted. While there was a bit of a blowout, with some of the medicine leaking, he got a good dose into the whale, who swam right on, seeming not even to notice."

The week after Haulena's attempt, Gaydos tried to administer a de-wormer through a dart gun to reduce any parasites Scarlet might be carrying (they'd found common parasites in her mother's scat). Gaydos didn't think parasites were Scarlet's main problem, but treating them might relieve some pressure on her immune system. Unfortunately, his shot failed to reach Scarlet. "It's nerve-wracking," Gaydos said. "Moving animal, moving boat. You do your best— that's all you can do."

In addition to medication delivered by Haulena, biologists from the Whale Sanctuary Project and Lummi Indian Nation tried a feeding trial. Eight live Chinook salmon slid into the water through a PVC pipe from the boat's deck toward Scarlet. Gaydos reported it didn't appear that Scarlet consumed any of the fish.

For those who knew Scarlet, it was difficult to watch her struggle. Taylor Shedd of Soundwatch, a boater-education program of San Juan Island's Whale Museum, couldn't imagine Scarlet in worse condition than she was in August. But by September, "she was even smaller and skinnier. There is some kind of internal drive to push forward and not give up."

Ultimately, all these efforts were unsuccessful, and Scarlet became more emaciated. She disappeared and was declared dead in early September. Unless they beach themselves, the bodies of dead whales are almost never recovered.

From her difficult birth and all through her short life, Scarlet was tenacious. The least we can do in her honor is persevere in protecting her threatened species.

CONFLICTED

We board the "Western Prince" on this final day of Marine
    Naturalist Training,
Hoping—
At least some of us—to spot J, K, and
L pods of Southern Resident killer whales.
Eyeing the gray horizon, squinting through raised binoculars,
We watch for a dorsal fin, a saddle patch, a slapping tail fluke.
And yet, I silently hope the killer whales avoid this boat and the
    other 111 vessels in operation,
Their engine din a threat to communication, blocking whale
Clicks and whistles calling their kin to swimming Chinook salmon.
Harbor seals, sea lions, and minke whales are the only mammals
    we see that day and
I confess, I'm relieved. Yes, it's thrilling to see Southern Residents
    in the wild, but
Not at their expense. Unless we change our ways, someday soon
    they'll all be
Gone.

BIRTH ANNOUNCEMENT

As the first anniversary of the COVID pandemic arrived, people around the world reflected on all that had transpired in a single year—a mere twelve months that seemed endless. One year earlier, many Americans had been traveling, gathering with friends and family to celebrate and grieve, commuting to their offices, and dining at their favorite restaurants. When someone was ill or needed surgery, they checked into the hospital, and loved ones sat at their bedsides. Wildfires, floods, and hurricanes had again forced acknowledgment of a climate crisis. Black Lives Matter rallies and protests continued (as did the racism that has plagued the world for centuries), a mob stormed the U.S. Capitol building, and a new president was inaugurated just after a Black, twenty-two-year-old woman poetically asked where we could find light "in this never-ending shade."

Even in the most devastating of times, people search for light—and often find it in unexpected places. In early September 2020, protectors of the Salish Sea found some light in news about J 35 (Tahlequah), a pregnant, thirty-two-year-old Southern Resident whale in J pod.

Researchers had learned on September 5 that J pod was in U.S. waters in the eastern Strait of Juan de Fuca. Another large group of the endangered Southern Resident killer whales was a few miles away in Canadian waters and swimming toward J pod. The Center for Whale Research on San Juan Island, Washington, launched three boats in hopes of finding a cluster of whales from J, K, and L pods, known as a "super-pod." The crew's goal: photo-identify every individual whale for a population census.

J pod, in its entirety, had returned to waters around San Juan Island on September 1 and remained in that area. The Center noted that Tahlequah and another pregnant whale, J41 (Eclipse), hadn't yet given birth. Then, on September 5, another report came in of the sighting of a very small calf. Researchers Dave Ellifrit and Katie Jones, plus veterinarian Dr. Sarah Bahan, went to check. They identified the mother as Tahlequah. Perhaps the super-pod seen September 1 had arrived to welcome its newest member, designated as J57.

This birth announcement brought joy around the world. After the mournful death of another of Tahlequah's calves in 2018, she'd carried the baby's body on her head for seventeen days while swimming about one thousand miles around the Salish Sea with her pod. It was termed a "Tour of Grief."

The Center crew knew the calf hadn't been born the day they saw it because the newborn's dorsal fin was upright; it takes a day or two to straighten after being bent over in the womb. Thus, they assigned September 4, 2020, as J57's birthday. They couldn't determine then whether the new calf was male or female, but they described it as "healthy and precocious, swimming vigorously alongside its mother in its second day of free-swimming life." Eventually, the Whale Museum would ask its members to vote for a name for Tahlequah's baby.

There's no scale or measuring tape at whale births in the wild, but the Center for Whale Research noted most newborn calves are seven to eight feet long and weigh three hundred to four hundred pounds (imagine writing *that* on a birth announcement). For the first year or two, an orca baby stays very close to its mother, swimming in her slipstream. Newborns suckle for short periods, dozens of times a day. Mother's milk is extremely rich, possibly containing forty to sixty percent fat. While calves may start experimenting with solid food at a young age, they typically don't fully wean until around the age of three.

Amidst the excitement of Tahlequah's baby, caution ruled. About forty percent of calves die early in life. This high mortality rate is related to reduced prey, especially the Chinook salmon Southern Residents favor; boat traffic noise that interferes with the whales' communication about food location; and pollutants such as PCBs— toxins pass from mother to calf during pregnancy and nursing. It's likely all three of these threats interact, increasing risks to these endangered whales.

Still, this birth announcement was cause to raise a glass to Tahlequah and her strength to carry a calf to term. And to toast her new, "precocious and healthy" baby, J57, eventually named Phoenix.

Conversations &

Correspondence

Real and Imagined

Slowly at first, one by one, door to door, through informal, then formal networks, people discovered they were all talking about the same thing: humanity and the environment are one. To connect the environment and human rights is an old refrain come 'round again. Reorchestrated for the times, it plays against the dissonance of a toxic and unjust world, and yet its message is the most hopeful I have heard in thirty-five years.

—PETER E SAUER
Research Scientist, Indiana University

A POSTHUMOUS INTERVIEW
WITH RACHEL CARSON

During my tenure as writer-in-residence on the Interisland ferry, I read at least as much as I wrote, filling the gaps in my knowledge about the Salish Sea and climate change. One author I read hungrily was Rachel Carson—marine scientist, writer, and editor. Perhaps best known for *Silent Spring* (1962), she also wrote two earlier books about the ocean. The first one, *Under the Sea-Wind* (1941) is an account of the interactions of a sea bird (a sanderling), a mackerel, and an eel off the Atlantic coast. *The Sea Around Us* (1951) serves as a biography of the sea and is noted for both its science and its poetic prose.

Carson was born in 1907 just upstream of the Allegheny River from heavily industrialized Pittsburgh, Pennsylvania. From her bedroom window, she could see smoke billow from the stacks of the American Glue Factory, which slaughtered horses. A graduate of Pennsylvania College for Women (now Chatham University), Carson studied at the Woods Hole Marine Biological Laboratory and received an MA in zoology from Johns Hopkins University. In *Silent Spring*, she continued writing about the interrelationship of all life and revealed the dangers of the pesticide DDT. After the book's publication, she was attacked by the chemical industry and accused by some government leaders as an alarmist. Testifying before Congress in 1963, Carson called for new policies to protect human health and the environment. She died in 1964 from breast cancer.

Although I didn't read Carson's work in its early days (my parents likely would have been in the "alarmist" camp and wouldn't have had the book on the coffee table), I know her writing inspired many to better understand the environment and to become its protectors. The Salish Sea desperately needs her right now.

I wish Rachel Carson were still around, perhaps joining me to ride and write on the *Tillikum*. I've read many of her words, and I've imagined what we would talk about. Author Kathleen Dean Moore "interviewed" Edward Abbey posthumously in *Great Tide Rising* (Counterpoint, 2016). I borrowed her technique, devising my own questions for Ms. Carson and using her previously-published words for her replies. I imagine the conversation going something like this.

———

IRIS GRAVILLE: You're a well-respected thinker and writer about conservation, Ms. Carson, and you spent a lot of time studying the sea. What drew you to the ocean?

RACHEL CARSON: As long as I can remember, it [the sea] has fascinated me. Even as a child—long before I had ever seen it—I used to imagine what it would look like, and what the surf sounded like. Since I grew up in an inland community, where we hadn't even a migrating seagull, I had to wait a long time to have my curiosity satisfied. As a matter of fact, it wasn't until I had graduated from college and gone to Woods Hole [Marine Biological Laboratory] ... that I saw the ocean. There, I began to get my first real understanding of the real sea world, that is, the world as it is known by shore-birds and fishes and beach crabs and all the other creatures that live in the sea or along its edge.[1]

All through the long history of Earth, it has been an area of un-
rest where waves have broken heavily against the land, where the
tides have pressed forward over the continents, receded, and then
returned.[2] Fish, amphibian, and reptile, warm-blooded bird and
mammal—each of us carries in our veins a salty stream in which the
elements sodium, potassium, and calcium are combined in almost
the same proportions as in seawater.[3]

IG: I live on an island on the Salish Sea in Washington State, and
I never tire of looking at the water's many shades of blue. But I'm
embarrassed to admit there's a great deal I don't know about this
body of water. For example, what makes it that color?

RC: The sea is blue because the sunlight is reflected back to our eyes
from the water molecules or from very minute particles suspended
in the sea. In the journey of the light rays downward into the water
and back to our eyes, all the red rays of the spectrum and most of
the yellow have been absorbed, so it is chiefly the cool, blue light
that we see.[4]

IG: I feel both fortunate to live so close to the sea and distressed
by the visible effects of climate change around me. But so many
people don't live anywhere near an ocean. Why should they care?

RC: Even in the vast and mysterious reaches of the sea, we are
brought back to the fundamental truth that nothing lives to itself.[5]
Water must be thought of in terms of the chains of life it supports.[6]

IG: At the centennial of your birth, forty-three years after your
death, the United States House of Representatives passed a resolution in your honor. Here's one portion of the resolution:

Resolved, That the House of Representatives—
recognizes that we could learn much from her today,
especially as we increasingly feel the effects

of climate change and consider measures to lessen
and eventually, reverse the impact it has on our planet.

What do you think is the most important learning we could
gain from you today?

RC: We also need to see the problem as a whole, to look beyond
the immediate and single event of the introduction of a pollutant
into the environment, and to trace the chain of events thus set into
motion. We must never forget the wholeness of that relationship.
We cannot think of the living organism alone; nor can we think
of the physical environment as a separate entity. The two exist together, each acting on the other to form an ecological complex
or an ecosystem. With these surface waters, through a series of
delicately adjusted, interlocking relationships, the life of all parts
of the sea is linked. What happens to a diatom in the upper, sunlit
strata of the sea may well determine what happens to a cod lying
on a ledge of some rocky canyon a hundred fathoms below, or to
a bed of multicolored, gorgeously plumed sea worms carpeting an
underlying shoal, or to a prawn creeping over the soft oozes of the
sea floor in the blackness of mile-deep water.[7]

IG: It appears the more we learn, the more complicated the natural
world is, and the more unattainable real change seems. How did we
get here, and how can we change?

RC: We behave, not like people guided by scientific knowledge,
but more like the proverbial bad housekeeper who sweeps the dirt
under the rug in the hope of getting it out of sight. We dump wastes
of all kinds into our streams, with the object of having them carried
away from our shores. We discharge the smoke and fumes of a million smokestacks and burning rubbish heaps into the atmosphere
in the hope that the ocean of air is somehow vast enough to contain
them. Now, even the sea has become a dumping ground, not only

for assorted rubbish, but for the poisonous garbage of the atomic age. And this is done, I repeat, without recognition of the fact that introducing harmful substances into the environment is not a one-step process. It is changing the nature of the complex ecological system and is changing it in ways that we usually do not foresee until it is too late. This lack of foresight is one of the most serious complications, I think. It is not half so important to know as to feel. The more clearly we can focus our attention on the wonders and realities of the universe about us, the less taste we shall have for destruction.[8]

IG: It can be difficult for people to believe that climate change is truly a crisis and that we humans are responsible for it. It's as if we're unwilling or afraid to look at the damage we've caused for decades and continue to wreak. How would you convince us to take this destruction seriously?

RC: I suppose it is rather a new, and almost a humbling thought, and certainly one born of this atomic age, that man could be working against himself. In spite of our rather boastful talk about progress and our pride in the gadgets of civilization, there is, I think, a growing suspicion—indeed, perhaps an uneasy certainty—that we have been sometimes a little too ingenious for our own good. In spite of the truly marvelous inventiveness of the human brain, we are beginning to wonder whether our power to change the face of nature should not have been tempered with wisdom for our own good, and with a greater sense of responsibility for the welfare of generations to come. Contrary to the beliefs that seem often to guide our actions, man does not live apart from the world; he lives in the midst of a complex, dynamic interplay of physical, chemical, and biological forces, and between himself and this environment there are continuing, never-ending interactions. One way to open your eyes is to ask yourself, "What if I had never seen this before? What if I knew I would never see it again?"[9]

IG: In 1952, you received the National Book Award for *The Sea Around Us*. At the time, it was described as poetic. Do you think of your writing as poetry?

RC: The winds, the sea, and the moving tides are what they are. If there is wonder and beauty and majesty in them, science will discover these qualities... If there is poetry in my book about the sea, it is not because I deliberately put it there, but because no one could write truthfully about the sea and leave out the poetry.[10]

IG: I'm deeply grateful for the work you did to raise awareness about the ocean, the danger of pesticides, and environmental protection. Writing personal essays and poems is my response to the climate crisis, but I often question if that's of any use. When did you decide to become a writer, and what are your thoughts about the value of creative writing?

RC: The aim of science is to discover and illuminate truth. And that, I take it, is the aim of literature. I can remember no time, even in earliest childhood, when I didn't assume I was going to be a writer.[11] A good deal of poetry and stories have been focused on the sea, and quite a bit of science as well. But the best writing combines the two. The books that influence—that push movements forward—are the books that marry science and emotion.[12]

IG: Every day, news reports about repealed environmental policies, extinction of animals, wildfires, oil spills, and rising seas cause fear and wear me (and many others) down. What advice can you offer to help us keep our spirits up?

RC: Wonder and humility are wholesome emotions, and they do not exist side by side with a lust for destruction.[13] Those who contemplate the beauty of the earth find reserves of strength that will last as long as life lasts. There is something infinitely healing in the repeated refrains of nature—the assurance that dawn comes after night and spring after winter.[14]

IG: How would you describe this present moment when it comes to the climate?

RC: We stand now where two roads diverge. But unlike the roads in Robert Frost's familiar poem, they are not equally fair. The road we have long been traveling is deceptively easy, a smooth super-highway on which we progress with great speed, but at its end lies disaster. The other fork of the road, the one less traveled by, offers our last, our only chance to reach a destination that assures the preservation of the earth.[15]

END NOTES

[1] Carson, Rachel. *The Sea Around Us.* Oxford: Oxford University Press, 1951.

[2] Carson, Rachel. *The Edge of the Sea.* New York: Houghton Mifflin, 1955.

[3] Carson, Rachel. *The Sea Around Us.* Oxford: Oxford University Press, 1951.

[5-6] Carson, Rachel. *Silent Spring.* New York: Houghton Mifflin, 1962.

[7] Carson, Rachel. *The Sea Around Us.* Oxford: Oxford University Press, 1951.

[8] Excerpt from acceptance speech for the John Burroughs Medal in 1952 for *The Sea*

[9] Carson, Rachel. *The Sense of Wonder.* New York: Harper Collins, 1956.

[10] Carson, Rachel. *The Sea Around Us.* Oxford: Oxford University Press, 1951.

[11] Lear, Linda, ed. *Lost Woods: The Discovered Writing of Rachel Carson.* Boston: Beacon Press, 1998.

[12] Excerpt from acceptance speech for the National Book Award in 1952 for *The Sea Around Us*

[13] Lear, Linda, ed. *Lost Woods: The Discovered Writing of Rachel Carson.* Boston: Beacon Press, 1998.

[14-15] Carson, Rachel. Silent Spring. New York: Houghton Mifflin, 1962.

WILD SEA DOCTOR

In YouTube videos by veterinarian Joseph K. Gaydos, you'll often hear him say, "It's wild!" The series, produced by the SeaDoc Society, is aptly named "Salish Sea Wild." No surprise, that's where you'll find Joe, a vet with a specialty in wild animal health.

Until Joe became the Science Director at SeaDoc in 2001, he'd lived and studied all over the world. Joe's parents both worked in public health, but it was his father's military career that took Joe from his birthplace in West Virginia to Maryland, Pennsylvania, Germany, and Japan. "I was fascinated with disease," Joe remembers, "but from day one, I was an animal person, catching snakes, lizards, and poisonous caterpillars. When I studied biology, I was fascinated with wildlife."

In 1986 while in college at Virginia Tech, Joe was an international exchange student in Kenya. He'd planned to attend veterinary school, but instead of beginning right after graduation in 1989, Joe and Julie Brunner, who soon became his wife, moved to a rain forest in Guatemala. For a year, the couple worked with children in an orphanage and lived on a river filled with long-tail otters. Joe's favorite word comes up again as he describes his time in Guatemala. "It was wild! They had a clinic but no doctor. They did have the book, *Where There Is No Doctor,* in Spanish. I used it to show me how to diagnose and treat malaria, stitch people up, and remove fish hooks—things like that."

After Joe graduated from veterinary school at the University of Pennsylvania in 1994, he and Julie were off again, this time to a wildlife park in southern Zimbabwe, on the border of Botswana and South Africa. "Half of my luggage was textbooks," Joe says. He likely needed them while working at the veterinary clinic there. While many of Joe's vet school friends were spaying cats, he remembers, "I was working on lions, black rhinos, and cheetahs." And the occasional human. "It was a long way to town, so people would come by our clinic with a machete wound," Joe says. "You just end up doing what you can do." Sounds like another wild time.

A year later, Joe and Julie moved back to West Virginia, and Joe joined a small, mixed-animal veterinary practice. "It was a real James Herriot experience. In the morning, I might take care of somebody's dog, and in the afternoon, I'd treat a prolapsed uterus in a cow. Weekends were just as busy, especially when it was calving time." Soon, Joe questioned if he wanted an eighty-hour work week. "I asked myself what was in my heart and realized I wanted to be working on wildlife conservation."

That meant another move in 1997 when Joe entered a Ph.D. program at the University of Georgia to study diseases in populations of wild animals. "They have an outstanding wildlife program there," Joe says. "I learned a lot of medicine, conservation, and biopolitics."

Biopolitics?

"Yeah, understanding how you get things done."

Joe couldn't know it at the time, but he was receiving the perfect education to feed his passion for wildlife conservation and prepare him for a position with the SeaDoc Society, a brand-new education and research organization on the Salish Sea.

The initial vision for SeaDoc came from Kathy and Ron McDowell when they moved to Orcas Island in 1996. As the McDowells learned more about the alarming decline of salmon, rockfish, shellfish, birds, and kelp and eelgrass beds in the Salish Sea, they wanted to see more science at work to improve conservation and increase collaboration between conservationists and scientists. Eventually, the couple contacted the University of California-Davis because of its renowned veterinary school and its Karen C. Drayer Wildlife Health Center. The University liked the McDowells' idea so much, it devoted $1.7 million to start the SeaDoc Society on Orcas Island in 2000.

Meanwhile, Joe thought SeaDoc might be a place he could put his doctoral studies to use, and besides, his wife had family in the West. He applied for the Science Director position, even though he didn't know how to scuba dive. Had no marine wildlife experience. Didn't know about sea stars. "They really took a chance on me. I guess it turned out okay," he says, flashing a smile that brightens his entire face. "I've been here nineteen years."

Since 2000, the SeaDoc Society has conducted and sponsored scientific research in this ecosystem that offers plenty to study: thirty-seven species of mammals, 172 types of birds, 253 species of fish, and more than three thousand varieties of invertebrates. Much of this wildlife is both threatened and cherished by the nearly eight million people living and working around the Salish Sea.

As Science Director, Joe looks for projects that impact policy or wildlife management. "I follow the questions and problems, talk to experts, and get them together to talk about action. We do projects where information will help us move toward a healthy eco-system. It's not just about whales, but also people, economics, and where we make our investments. That's where science meets policy."

Although Joe doesn't consider himself a whale biologist, he worked with others at SeaDoc on the first-ever attempt to treat a sick killer whale, J50 (Scarlet), in the spring of 2018. "We had started to think about what we'd do with an entangled whale or a whale with infection. We've done this kind of care with gorillas for decades," Joe said, referring to SeaDoc's sister program, Gorilla Doctors. They've provided health care for endangered mountain gorillas in central Africa since the mid-1980s and partnered with the UC Davis School of Veterinary Medicine in 2009.

When it came to Scarlet, though, "the public was all over the place," Joe says. "Half said we should quit experimenting, and the other half said we had to do more." Despite reviewing her history, visual and behavioral assessments, and evaluation of breath and fecal samples, Joe and other scientists never identified a cause for Scarlet's sickness. Consequently, their care focused on administering medications to treat potential secondary infections such as bacterial pneumonia and parasites. Sadly, the treatment didn't work for Scarlet; she died that fall.

But, Joe believes, "treating free-range wildlife isn't a long-term solution. It's mitigation. We need to be recovering salmon, worrying about vessel noise, and reducing human-made contamination."

How does Joe cope with the urgency of these worries? "There are days you can be down, and days you can be up. I was on the Governor's Task Force for whale recovery. It was nice to see the state play a role and to work with British Columbia." But, the biopolitics of a task force don't move quickly. "A lot of recommendations came out in years one and two, and they're still being worked on," Joe says. "I hope every day when I go to work that we're going to get ahold of this."

Clearly, Joe finds much in his work that sustains his hope. "I love the animals, being in the water, under the water [yes, he did learn to scuba dive], thinking about them and helping them," he says. "And the people I get to work with—I've learned so much from all of them. It's amazing to be part of something bigger than yourself."

Two of those "bigger than yourself" accomplishments involved a different kind of writing than Joe's typical research reports. In 2015, Joe and geologist and naturalist Audrey D. Benedict co-authored *The Salish Sea; Jewel of the Pacific Northwest.* Over fifty-five photographers contributed color images of sea life, and editor Alice Levine and book designer Annie Douden made major contributions to the hard-cover. Joe and Audrey also created a companion book, *Explore the Salish Sea: A Nature Guide for Kids.* Joe's delighted that, with the help of additional fundraising, SeaDoc has "sent thousands of books to Title I schools, tribal schools, and summer programs."

Joe's motive with both books was to get more people connected and, thus, committed to protecting the Salish Sea.

I ask Joe about the successes he's most proud of in his work. "I think a lot of the stuff I've been able to do…" he pauses and tears up, "it's not me, but a lot of people." Joe takes a deep breath. "Persistence," he continues. "And still moving ahead in the face of fear. That's the biggest thing for me—have the guts to go forward, and if you make a mistake, apologize and go again. Don't be afraid to try something. If it doesn't work, don't beat yourself up. Make a new plan."

For Joe, "this is hard—this kind of change. Ruckleshaus [William Ruckelshaus, the first director of the Environmental Protection Agency] once told me, 'If things were easy, we would have already done this. It's going to take time, a long time.' You can decimate a population quickly, but recovering it takes longer." Then, Joe's persistence rises again. "But I think we'll get a new contract, a new ocean ethic."

The Salish Sea isn't the only place Joe follows the ethic of restoration and conservation. "I grow Garry oak trees from plants in my yard every year. My wife teases me, 'You won't see it.' And I say, but somebody will!"

Won't that be wild?

IMAGINED CONVERSATION
BETWEEN RACHEL CARSON AND
GRETA THUNBERG

What if Rachel Carson and Greta Thunberg were to meet today? I like to imagine moderating a conversation between the two women, all three of us sitting in Adirondack chairs on a stretch of rocky beach beside the Salish Sea. As a chilly breeze ruffles the blue-gray water, steam rises from our mugs of herbal tea.

I can't know what these two climate activists would discuss if they met in the twenty-first century. But, modifying the form I used in my "conversation" with Rachel Carson, I've prepared questions I'd ask of the two women. For their answers, I drew from their writing and speeches as well as what others have written about them.

Greta Thunberg, an eighteen-year-old from Sweden, stands barely five feet tall. She seems even smaller when on a stage before hundreds of people or being pursued by dozens of photographers. For our meeting, she wears her standard outfit: jeans, a T-shirt and a hoodie, and tennis shoes; her light brown hair is parted in the middle and braided.

Rachel Carson grew up in rural Pennsylvania. Her brown hair in tight curls frames her face. Just as in many photographs of this writer, scientist, and ecologist, she's wearing a white blouse with a dark suit jacket and skirt. Biographies portray Ms. Carson as solemn and reserved with a forthright gaze, not given to quick smiles. She's petite, like Ms. Thunberg, and speaks so softly I have to strain to hear her.[1] However, I suspect if Ms. Carson could read the 2019 compilation of Ms. Thunberg's speeches, she'd probably agree with its title, *No One Is Too Small to Make a Difference.*

The two activists share more than diminutive stature. Ms. Carson began writing stories (often involving animals) at age eight. Her first publication came when she was ten and won the Silver Badge from the respected children's magazine, *St. Nicholas.*[2] Ms. Thunberg's eighth year was an important one for her, too. That's how old she was when she began thinking about climate change and wondering why adults weren't working to alleviate it. At fifteen, she won a writing competition about the environment, and her essay was published in a Swedish newspaper.[3]

In other ways, however, Ms. Thunberg's and Ms. Carson's experiences have been quite different. According to a 2016 story about Ms. Carson in the *Pittsburgh Post-Gazette*, she published pieces under the byline "R.L. Carson" to reduce the chance readers would dismiss her pro-environment message if they knew the writer was a woman.

Many people know Ms. Thunberg by her first name. When Penguin published her book of speeches, the white cover blared GRETA in black ink and in all caps in a bold, seventy-point typeface.

Time Magazine named Ms. Thunberg the 2019 "Person of the Year" and described her this way:

"She has Asperger's syndrome, which means she doesn't operate on the same emotional register as many of the people she meets. She dislikes crowds; ignores small talk; and speaks in direct, uncomplicated sentences...Where others smile to cut the tension,

Thunberg is withering. Where others speak the language of hope, Thunberg repeats the unassailable science: Oceans will rise. Cities will flood. Millions of people will suffer."[4]

A half-century before *Time* recognized Ms. Thunberg, that same magazine called Rachel Carson's *Silent Spring* "unfair, one-sided, hysterically over-emphatic and filled with oversimplifications and downright errors." Its review of the book included denials of its accuracy by a toxicologist and other "respected experts" from the U.S. Public Health Service and the National Academy of Sciences, among others, as well as the Assistant Surgeon General. [5]

Let's hear what the two women have to say about the joys and struggles of being well-known environmental activists.

—

IRIS GRAVILLE: Rachel, Greta, it's a great pleasure to meet both of you and to talk with you about your lives and your work.

Rachel, let's begin with you. Even though many people, Greta included, have read your books and know about your long struggle to prohibit the pesticide DDT, can you tell us what drove you to write about the environment?

RACHEL CARSON: First, let me say to Greta, I'm delighted to meet you. I admire your efforts and the way you've inspired thousands of people of all ages to recognize the catastrophe of human effects on the environment and demand change. [Greta's solemn demeanor turns to a grin.]

I studied English in college, but a course in biology changed all that.[6] The more I learned about the use of pesticides, the more appalled I became. I realized that here was the material for a book. What I discovered was that everything which meant most to me as a naturalist was being threatened and that nothing I could do would be more important.[7]

Even in the 1960s, we had persisted too long in the kind of thinking that may have been appropriate in the days of pioneers, but is so no longer—the assumption that the rivers, atmosphere, and the sea are vast enough to contain whatever we pour in them.[8]

IG: Rachel, in your day, people spoke of your efforts as conservation and ecology. Now we use terms like climate change and climate crisis. Greta, will you describe what you've been doing in response to the current crisis?

GRETA THUNBERG: Thank you. Hello, Rachel, I'm honored to meet you. [Rachel softens her usually compressed lips into a gentle smile.] I appreciate the way you spoke out about the sea and pesticides in the 1960s.

I come from Sweden, and I speak on behalf of future generations. In 2018, I sat alone in front of Parliament every Friday, on strike from school to show my concern about the climate. Now, thousands of other students from all around the world do the same. Many people don't want to listen to us; they say we're just children. But we're only repeating the message of the united climate science.[9]

Adults keep saying: "We owe it to the young people to give them hope." And I say, but I don't want your hope. I don't want you to be hopeful. I want you to panic. I want you to feel the fear I feel every day. And then I want you to act. I want you to act as you would in a crisis. I want you to act as if our house is on fire. Because it is.[10]

IG: Greta, millions of youth stand with you in your work. For example, four million people, many of them teens, joined the global climate strike on September 20, 2019. What do your parents think of your actions?

GT: When I told my parents about my plan, they weren't very fond of it. They did not support the idea of school striking, and they said that if I were to do this, I would have to do it completely by myself and with no support from them.[11] My parents were as far from climate activists as possible before I made them aware of the situation.[12]

IG: And other adults? What do they say? I know you've addressed heads of state at the United Nations, met with the Pope, and that Margaret Atwood compared you to Joan of Arc.[13]

GT: One of the funniest reactions was a Tweet by President Donald Trump in response to *Time Magazine* naming me "Person of the Year" for 2019. He posted: *So ridiculous. Greta must work on her anger management problem, then go to a good old-fashioned movie with a friend! Chill Greta, Chill!*[14]

So, I changed the personal biography on my Twitter account to read: "A teenager working on her anger management problem. Currently chilling and watching a good old-fashioned movie with a friend."[15]

IG: Rachel, I'm guessing you're happy you didn't have to deal with Twitter. There are many new ways people communicate now. It's called "social media," but not everyone who uses it is very social. But in your time, there were plenty of people who didn't want to listen to your warnings, and others undermined them. How did you deal with the criticism?

RC: Hundreds of thousands of dollars were spent to not only discredit my book, *Silent Spring*, but also the hysterical woman who wrote it. Fortunately [a soft chuckle slips out], the attacks seemed to backfire, creating more publicity than my publisher ever could have afforded. I was also accused of communist sympathies, of being a peace nut, a fanatic, even a woman. A former Secretary of the Department of Agriculture asked, "Why is a spinster with no children concerned with genetics?" One reviewer claimed, "Her book is more poisonous than the pesticides she condemns." The attacks weren't pleasant, but they didn't really get to me.[16]

There *were* supporters, even though magazines and newspapers that ran favorable reviews were told they'd lose advertising.[17]

IG: You may not know this, Rachel, but *Silent Spring* was translated into many languages and it still sells more than twenty-five thousand copies every year.[18] [Another slight grin from Rachel.]

How about you, Greta? How is it for you when people say unkind things about you?

GT: I don't care about being popular, I care about climate justice and the living planet.[19] Many people love to spread rumors saying that I have people "behind me" or that I'm being "paid" or "used" to do what I'm doing. But there is no one "behind" me except for myself.[20]

IG: Greta, you're very skilled at speaking about the urgency to act as we would in a crisis. I'm sure people ask you how a young person like you can put so much attention on this subject. I think age doesn't matter, but I do wonder how you have such strength and commitment.

GT: It is hard to be different sometimes. I have Asperger's, so I'm on the autism spectrum. Many people see it as a weakness or disease, but it's not. I'm in some ways grateful for my diagnosis; if my brain worked differently, I wouldn't be able to sit for hours and read things I'm interested in.[21]

IG: Your father has said when you were eleven years old, you fell into a deep depression about climate change. For months, you stopped speaking almost entirely and ate so little you were nearly hospitalized.

GT: Yes. My parents took time off work to nurse me through what my father calls a period of "endless sadness." I just remember feeling confused. I couldn't understand how that could exist, that existential threat, and yet we didn't prioritize it. I was maybe in a bit of denial, like, "That can't be happening, because if that were happening, then the politicians would be taking care of it." While learning about climate change triggered my depression in the first place, it was also what got me out of my depression because there were things I could do to improve the situation. I don't have time to be depressed anymore. [22]

IG: I'm glad to hear that, Greta. I know that, despite how desperate the climate crisis is, many people who feel sadness and fear are eased when they act.

What wisdom can the two of you offer to help us all keep going?

RC: If I had influence with the good fairy who is supposed to preside over the christening of all children, I should ask that her gift to each child in the world be a sense of wonder so indestructible that it would last throughout life, as an unfailing antidote against … boredom and disenchantment … the sterile preoccupation with things that are artificial, the alienation from the sources of our strength.[23]

Those who contemplate the beauty of the earth find reserves of strength that will endure as long as life lasts. I believe that natural beauty has a necessary place in the development of any individual or any society.[24]

GT: We often talk about these negative tipping points, things we can't change. There could be also positive tipping points, like when people say they've had enough. The tipping point we're waiting for right now is when people will understand the power we actually have. I'd like to tell my grandchildren that we did everything we could. That we did it for them and for the generations to come.[25]

IG: Thank you, Greta and Rachel, for sharing your thoughts and for your words of hope. I'm glad you were able to meet each other, even if it was only in my imagination. You both inspire me.

END NOTES

[1-2]   Lear, Linda, ed. *Lost Woods: The Discovered Writing of Rachel Carson.* Boston: Beacon Press. 2011(Kindle Edition).

[3-4]   Edward Felsenthal, "Time 2019 Person of the Year, Greta Thunberg," *Time Magazine* December 4, 2019.

[5]   "Pesticides, the Price for Progress," *Time Magazine,* Sept. 28, 1962.

[6]   Lear, Linda, ed. *Lost Woods: The Discovered Writing of Rachel Carson.* Boston: Beacon Press. 2011(Kindle Edition).

[7]   Carson, Rachel, Dorothy Freeman, Martha E. Freeman. *Always, Rachel: The Letters of Rachel Carson and Dorothy Freeman, 1952-1964.* Boston: Beacon Press.

[8]   Lear, Linda, ed. *Lost Woods: The Discovered Writing of Rachel Carson.* Boston: Beacon Press. 2011(Kindle Edition).

[9-12]   Thunberg, Greta. *No One is Too Small to Make a Difference.* New York: Penguin Press. 2019.

[13]   Edward Felsenthal, "Time 2019 Person of the Year, Greta Thunberg," *Time Magazine* December 4, 2019.

[14]   Donald Trump (@realDonaldTrump,) "So ridiculous," Twitter, December 11, 2019.

[15]   Madeline Roth, "Chill! Greta Thunberg Flips Script on Trump by Telling Him to Work on His Anger Management Problem," *The Independent* December 12, 2019.

[16]   *Sense of Wonder,* one-woman play about Rachel Carson, written and performed by Kaiulani Lee, excerpted on "Bill Moyers' Journal: Rachel Carson's Legacy," Season 11, Episode 24, PBS.

[17]   Lear, Linda, ed. *Lost Woods: The Discovered Writing of Rachel Carson.* Boston: Beacon Press. 2011(Kindle Edition).

[18]   *Sense of Wonder,* one-woman play about Rachel Carson, written and performed by Kaiulani Lee, excerpted on "Bill Moyers' Journal: Rachel Carson's Legacy," Season 11, Episode 24, PBS.

[19-20]   Thunberg, Greta. *No One is Too Small to Make a Difference.* New York: Penguin Press. 2019.

[21-22]   Edward Felsenthal, "Time 2019 Person of the Year, Greta Thunberg," *Time Magazine* December 4, 2019.

[23]   Carson, Rachel. *The Sense of Wonder.* New York: Harper Collins, 1956.

24 Lear, Linda, ed. *Lost Woods: The Discovered Writing of Rachel Carson.* Boston: Beacon Press. 2011(Kindle Edition).

25 Edward Felsenthal, "Time 2019 Person of the Year, Greta Thunberg," *Time Magazine* December 4, 2019.

EVERYBODY LOVES
A POOPING WHALE

Dr. Deborah Giles knows how to get an audience's attention. She often grabs it with magnificent slides of Southern Resident killer whales swimming in pods, diving for salmon, or gathering in greeting ceremonies. Sometimes it's the devastating statistics she reports about dwindling numbers of the Southern Residents in the Salish Sea that lead people to scribble notes. The best proclamation I've heard her make, though, was in a video recording of her talk at the World Salmon Forum in Seattle in 2019.

"Everybody loves a pooping whale."

The video picked up chuckles from the crowd, but Giles's serious look remained unchanged until she explained the significance of whale stool. "It means you have an eating whale," she said with a smile. It turns out, Giles (she goes by her last name, pronounced *jylz*) knows a lot about whale poop. She serves as a research biologist for the University of Washington's (UW) Center for Conservation Biology and the Science and Research Director for the nonprofit, Wild Orca.

"The program was the brainchild of Dr. Sam Wasser," Giles told me during a Zoom interview from her home office in 2021. "In

1997, he started to use scent-detecting dogs to locate fecal samples of endangered species." Wasser, Director of the UW Center for Conservation Biology, had done similar work in the Redwoods with spotted owls. Through his Conservation Canines Program, he collaborated with Sgt. Barbara Davenport, Master Canine Trainer with the Washington State Department of Corrections. The pair modified narcotics detection dog methods to train dogs to locate stool from threatened and endangered species.

Not just any dog can work in the program, though. The Conservation Canines website describes the ideal scat detection dog as "intensely focused with an insatiable urge to play. Their obsessive, high-energy personalities make them difficult to maintain as a family pet, so they often end up at a shelter." Giles explained these dogs have such energy, they're happy to work eight hours for the reward of playing with a ball after successfully locating whale poop.

Giles's own dog, Eba, a stocky, thirty-pound mixed breed her sister rescued, has just that drive.

"Lead dog handlers Julianne Ubigau and Tammy Rock suggested Eba would be good at finding scat," Giles said. Over the course of a few days working with these two trainers, she learned how to locate whale scat samples hidden on land. Giles beamed as she told me, "On Eba's second day on the water, she found her first wild whale scat sample on her own."

Since 2009, Giles has been the vessel captain for the whale feces detection dogs' research boat. In 2019, she moved to the front of the boat to be Eba's handler. Eba, in her own dog-size life jacket, stands in the bow of the research boat and sniffs for the scent she's been trained to identify. Wasser compares the dogs' ability to detect a specific scent to one of us being able to taste a teaspoon of sugar in a million gallons of water.

In an interview on CNN in December 2020, Giles described the scat-scouting work as consisting of a "three-being team. It's a coordinated dance between the dog reacting to a scent, the handler being able to interpret that change in body behavior of the dog, and then the boat driver really being in tune with not only the dog and the handler but also all of the other things associated with being on the water."

Giles seems to love talking about the team and its work. Her smile broadened, and she started to talk faster. "The dog is on the front of the boat just kind of hanging out and sniffing, and then when she gets a hit, she has a pretty massive behavior change." Giles described how her own dog responds. "Eba will start whining, licking her lips, and heading toward the direction of the scent." When that happens, Giles uses hand signals to communicate Eba's intentions to the driver, who guides the boat perpendicular to the wind up to a quarter of a mile behind or parallel to the whales. Often the driver has to zig-zag to follow Eba's directions to find the mucusy poop moving in relation to the currents. The sample often resembles a combination of algae and snot as it moves along with the water.

The team has to work quickly when the dogs detect the scat because it can start to sink within a few minutes. Scientists scoop it out of the water and send it to Wasser's lab for analysis. "Dogs never have to go near any endangered animals," Giles said. And the feces yield much information about the whales' health. "We can measure DNA, diet, hormones, pathogens, toxicants, and pregnancy noninvasively," Giles explained. Those indicators help measure species abundance and distribution, resource use, and physiological health.

Although it's unlikely Giles ever imagined the work she's committed to today, there were signs in childhood she'd end up caring for animals in some way. Soon after the day a young Giles and her dad removed a spider from their bathtub, Giles dreamed she could switch places with a whale being held in captivity so the whale could experience freedom. "My dad really valued animals," she said. "He taught us an ethic about animals that set the course for my whole life."

At age eight, Giles remembers, she drew a picture of a killer whale. "I probably saw one for the first time in a book," she said. "My family didn't have a TV." From then on, Giles felt a connection with whales. By the time she had her driver's license, she was out leafletting against keeping whales in captivity, including Tokitae, a Southern Resident killer whale captured in 1970 with five other juvenile orcas. They were all sold and transported from the Salish

Sea to "marine parks" around the world. Tokitae, whose stage name is Lolita, has been performing at the Miami Seaquarium for over fifty years.

For Giles's eighteenth birthday, friends took her from her home in Sacramento, California, to San Juan Island to see the whales she treasured. On the way to an island campground, they saw a pod of whales heading north along the shoreline. They stopped right in the middle of the road to watch. That was the first of many annual visits by Giles to the San Juan Islands.

"I knew I had to do some work to help these killer whales," Giles said. One summer while visiting San Juan, Giles attended a talk by Albert Shepard, curator at the Whale Museum. Later on that visit, she went to talk with him. "He challenged me to quit my job and do an internship at the museum." In 2005, Giles did just that. A couple of years later, she started a doctoral program at the University of California, Davis with a focus on Southern Residents. In 2009, she joined Sam Wasser's canine project and went on to complete her Ph.D. in 2014. Along the way, her research was cited in Washington State regulations in 2012 requiring that boats stay two hundred yards away from the Southern Residents. "That's a conservation biologist's dream to have your work used for policy," Giles said.

Giles didn't hesitate when I asked her about one of the most important lesson she's learned as a conservation biologist. "We've damaged the environment," she said, and the responsibility to repair it "is entirely up to us." She also suggested we should be more like the Southern Residents. "They give us an example of a more pure way of living in the natural world," Giles said. "They hunt collaboratively, care for each other when another is sick, literally, hold each other up. We could learn from the whales' deep, deep sense of family and community."

That seems like something else everybody could love.

POSTCARD FROM WILD ORCAS

From:
The Salish Sea
48.3295° N, 123.1407° W
Washington State
U.S.A.

To:
Shorelines Hearing Board
PO Box 40903
Olympia, WA 98504

October 2, 2018

Dear Members of the Shorelines Hearings Board,

Your "Yes" to permits for the Anacortes Marathon Oil Refinery expansion last week ignored 7,500 human voices that speak for us. We live from spring to fall in the inland waters of the Salish Sea. We know your plans to send 120 more tankers carrying petrochemicals through here per year means more threats to our saltwater home.

Increased traffic raises the risk for toxic oil spills, deadly for the Chinook salmon that feed us.

The roar of your tankers scrambles our clicks, whistles and calls, confusing communication with our kin. How can we signal each other about food and hazards?

Could you hear our voices when you met? Our grieving tones are different than the spout of air between dives in search of food. They're more like moans as we watch our young ones shrink, their bodies turning peanut-shaped from starvation.

This isn't the last time you'll hear from us.

Sincerely,
The Remaining 73 Southern Resident killer whales

THANK YOU NOTE
FROM THE ORCAS
OCTOBER 12, 2019

10-12-19

Dear Thurston County Superior Court,

We are fin-slapping and spy-hopping with joy! Unlike two other courts before you, you saw that Marathon Oil Refinery's expansion in Anacortes didn't follow the Shorelines Management Act to protect us and other marine life. Hurray to you for understanding the project would damage our summer home, the Salish Sea.

We expected the Shorelines Hearings Board to notice Marathon's plan threatens our health. The refinery expansion would swell the risk of oil spills, emit greenhouse gases equal to seventy thousand more cars on the road each year, and intensify tanker traffic noise that messes with our hunt for food.

Thank goodness you didn't ignore how the project would endanger our very survival.

We appreciate you didn't fall for Marathon's evidence from a forestry biologist based in Portland, Oregon about the safety of the expansion. Really? The Board believed a tree expert understands how this plan would hurt orca whales?

We've been through this before and know there are bound to be more appeals. Can we count on you to put the environment (and us) before noisy, toxic businesses? Our lives depend on it.

With gratitude,
The Salish Sea's remaining 73 Southern Resident Orca Whales

Hope

The biggest gift you can give is to be absolutely present, and when you're worrying about whether you're hopeful or hopeless or pessimistic or optimistic, who cares? The main thing is that you're showing up, that you're here and that you're finding ever more capacity to love this world because it will not be healed without that. That is what is going to unleash our intelligence and our ingenuity and our solidarity for the healing of our world.

—JOANNA MACY

ENVIRONMENTALISM
MEETS ANTI-RACISM

Vogue Magazine isn't a publication I've ever turned to for news about the environment. That is, until a blogger directed me to an essay in the June 8, 2020 issue—"Why Every Environmentalist Should Be Anti-racist." The essay's author, Leah Thomas, is a 2017 graduate of Chapman University with a bachelor's degree in Environmental Science and Policy. She's one of many Black, Indigenous, People of Color (BIPOC) environmentalists talking about the connection between climate and racism.

"In my environmental science classes—where I was often met with confusion when I tried my best to advocate for the protection of people of color—I was shocked," Thomas writes, "to find the very clear data that communities of color have been most exposed to poor air quality and environmental conditions. I realized my work could directly contribute to the fight against racism."

Thomas drew on Kimberlé Crenshaw's work in 1989 on the intersection of race and sex and contends our overlapping identities all intersect in some way. Thomas uses the term intersectional environmentalism to describe "...an inclusive version of environmentalism that advocates for both the protection of people and the planet. It identifies the ways in which injustices happening to marginalized communities and the earth are interconnected. It brings injustices done to the most vulnerable communities, and the earth, to the forefront and does not minimize or silence social inequality. The time is now to examine the ways the Black Lives Matter movement and environmentalism are linked."

Just days after George Floyd's murder in Minneapolis on May 25, 2020, *New York Times* columnist Somini Sengupta interviewed Black climate activists about the connections between racism and climate change. Her article, "Black Environmentalists Talk About Climate and Anti-Racism," features three prominent environment defenders—Robert D. Bullard, Sam Grant, and Heather McGhee—and their views that the climate movement can be anti-racist.

Bullard, a professor at Texas Southern University, often described as the "father of environmental justice," has written for more than thirty years about the need to redress environmental racism. "The rich have a bigger carbon footprint than the poor, but it is the poor who are more likely to be people of color in this country and who are often most vulnerable to the impact of climate change. The people who are feeling the worst impacts of climate, their voices have got to be heard."

Grant, executive director of MN350.org, the Minnesota affiliate of the international climate activist group 350.org, believes "...part of our challenge as an organization focused on the climate crisis is to honor what's primary for people and through dialogue and through relationships, help people see the connection between that issue and the broader climate crisis. So, it's not choosing this or that. Or this, then that. It's this and that."

McGhee is a senior fellow at Demos, a nonpartisan research and advocacy group, and the author of *The Sum of Us: What Racism Costs Everyone and How We Can Prosper Together*. She suggests an anti-racist climate movement should be led by "a real multiracial coalition that endorses environmental justice principles; its goals should seek to uplift the most vulnerable."

Another voice calling for intersectional environmentalism is Hop Hopkins of the Sierra Club. He wrote in the organization's June 2020 newsletter about "How Racism is Killing the Planet" and presented a long-overdue realization growing in the environmental movement. "You can't have climate change without sacrifice zones, and you can't have sacrifice zones without disposable people, and you can't have disposable people without racism." To put it even more succinctly, Hopkins says, "We'll never stop climate change without ending white supremacy."

Like most people I know, I often feel overwhelmed by three intersecting crises pulling me to act: racism, climate change, and COVID-19. Writing nonfiction is the form of activism I'm most drawn to, and I turn to other writers, like Ijeoma Oluo and Camille T. Dungy, for wisdom and inspiration in my work. In *So You Want to Talk About Race,* Oluo describes intersectionality as "the belief that our social justice movements must consider all of the intersections of identity, privilege, and oppression that people face in order to be just and effective."

Poet and essayist Dungy makes a good case in the affirmative in her *Georgia Review* essay, "Is All Writing Environmental Writing?"

"We are in the midst of the planet's sixth great extinction," Dungy writes, "in a time where we are seeing the direct effects of radical global climate change via more frequent and ferocious storms, hotter drier years accompanied by more devastating wildfires, snow where there didn't used to be snow, and less snow where permafrost used to be a given. Yet some people prefer to maintain categories for what counts as environmental writing and what is historical writing or social criticism or biography and so on. I can't compartmentalize my attentions."

I'm learning from these and other activists who make the connections between racism and the climate crisis just how interrelated these pressing issues are. Like Dungy, I'm discovering I can't confine my environmental writing to narrative prose, as I've typically done for many subjects. As I write about the climate crisis and its effects on the Salish Sea, environmental justice, and health, I'm drawn to poetry, lists, profiles, and metaphor. More and more, I strive for all of my writing to be environmental writing

This exploration, spurred by the article in *Vogue*, taught me something else. My assumption that a fashion magazine wouldn't be concerned about racism or the environment is inaccurate. Unexpectedly, *Vogue* opened my mind and heart further to intersectional environmentalism. And thanks to Leah Thomas for not limiting where she takes her message— "To fight for social justice is to fight for the protection of the environment and vice versa."

Hopefully, in the future, there will be more white voices joining these intersecting causes.

LESSONS

1. OUR TIME

On the first vessel run of the Interisland this autumn day, I gather with deck hands in the ferry galley after the final trucks and cars are loaded. Some of the crew pump steaming coffee out of a tall, black thermos on the counter. Talk today is about enjoying the quiet of the morning now that the tourists have returned home and most of the drivers and walk-ons are regulars.

This is *our* time now, and I feel that sense of entitlement— *our* time, *our* boat, *our* Salish Sea.

2. OWNERSHIP

I fuss and fume silently over the sense of ownership, and I wonder. Who owns the sea? What does the sea own? Why do we even put any thought into owning what is just here, available and necessary for us although we aren't so necessary for it?

Except now that we've destroyed so much of the life below and above the water-line.

3. IMAGINATION

In my imagination, I follow you, *Orcinus orca,* as you dive deeper into the sea than I've ever been before, into a darkness darker than I've ever known, so dark I can barely see your white eye patch gleaming against your silky, black skin, and I can only feel the other creatures under the water, swimming with you and with me, creatures you know well, but I'm just getting to know even though they're here all the time.

At least for now.

4. RENEWAL

In the Interisland ferry's main cabin, signs with red letters and diagrams explain the steps in case of an emergency. For the Salish Sea, and for us, the emergency alarm has already been sounded. We need to take lessons from the orca pods. Travel together in tight groups, some swimming and diving ahead in search of food to pass along to those with fewer reserves. Sleep together in a cove in moonlight. Celebrate being back together after a time apart. Carry our dead as long as we need to, mourn their loss, and then somehow return to frolic.

And maybe feel a glimmer of renewal, of hope, to carry on.

BABY PICTURES

In March 2021, a friend e-mailed photos of her newborn son. The young mother's parents (the baby's grandparents) sent pictures, too. They included many mutual friends on the mailings, as there was a large circle of us awaiting news of this birth. And what a thrill it was to see a healthy mom and a healthy baby.

My feelings of intense joy for this young family are built on decades of friendship with the mom and her parents. Surprisingly, my responses to the births of three Southern Resident killer whales bore some resemblance to this news of a human birth. All four newborns—human and whale—spark happiness and hope for me.

My happy, hopeful emotions began on September 5, 2020, with the notice that thirty-two-year-old J35 (Tahlequah) had given birth to a son, J57 (Phoenix). He was also welcomed by an older brother, J47 or Notch. Tahlequah had caught the world's attention two years earlier when her previous calf died shortly after birth, and she carried its four-hundred-pound body as she swam for seventeen days. Her new baby, Phoenix, was described as precocious at birth; nearly six months later, he continued to look healthy, according to the Center for Whale Research. Researcher Katie Jones took photos of the robust infant.

A few weeks after Phoenix's birth, J41 (Eclipse) gave birth to J58 (Crescent). Eclipse is fifteen years old and also has a son, J51 (Nova). The sex of Eclipse's newborn wasn't determined when first spotted, but everyone was hoping for a girl. More females (cows) are needed to increase the possibility of births of this endangered species. A baby picture by Talia Goodyear of Orca Spirit Adventures showed Crescent swimming alongside Eclipse. In mid-March 2021, researchers discovered that Crescent is a female.

Then, just before my friend's baby arrived, thirty-year-old L86 lived up to her name—Surprise!—when whale researchers discovered she'd given birth. This newborn, L125, is a welcome addition to L pod, which hasn't had a birth since January 2019. It is the fourth calf born to Surprise! A male, Pooka (L106), born in 2005, is still alive. Victoria (L112), born in 2009, was killed in 2012 by blunt force trauma, possibly during military exercises. Another of L86's babies, L120, died at seven weeks in 2014.

Dave Elllifrit, a photo identification expert at the Center for Whale Research, posted pictures showing that L125 matched his description of "nicely filled out . . . perfectly normal." And, since all three Southern Resident pods (J, K, and L) were in Haro Strait the day L125 was photographed, Ellifrit could confirm that J pod babies Phoenix and Eclipse "looked to be doing well."

Congratulations to these parents and their new babies. I'm eager for more updates—and pictures—of all of them.

THE SALISH SEA'S RIGHT
TO SURVIVE AND THRIVE

There's a danger in believing humans are separate from nature. More people around the globe recognize that. The Rights of Nature movement is contributing to this awareness as supporters work to correct systems that treat corporations as people and nature as property to be bought and sold. The movement's efforts build on millennia-old Indigenous understandings that nature and natural entities have the right to thrive and survive. Some, however, view the rights-based approach as radical.

Radical is a label many residents of San Juan County, Washington wear with pride. The Pacific Northwest county's over four hundred islands and nearly seventeen thousand residents are surrounded by the Salish Sea, one of the world's largest inland seas. The sea's name pays tribute to the first inhabitants of the region, the Coast Salish. San Juan County's strong stewardship ethic has resulted in a variety of "radical" efforts such as recycling centers on the four ferry-served islands, land and water conservation and preservation efforts, affordable housing initiatives, and hundreds of thriving nonprofits to address resident needs.

In 2005, voters agreed to create a county Home Rule charter so they could have more input on governance. This decision made

San Juan County the smallest and the sixth in the state to adopt a charter (a seventh county did the same in 2015). In 2020, county voters elected a review commission to consider amendments to the Home Rule document, an opportunity the county has every fifteen years. One of those commissioners is also a member of Community Rights San Juan Islands (CRSJI), a local organization working to recognize in law the Rights of Nature and, specifically, the Rights of the Salish Sea.

The CRSJI group promotes respecting nature's right to exist, thrive, and regenerate vital life cycles. It follows the Rights of Nature's "legal framework to bridge ancient recognition of our human place in the web of life and our modern legal system and to shift our view of nature as property to one that recognizes and respects nature as rights-bearing."

The main concerns CRSJI hopes a San Juan County Rights of Nature law would address include protecting and fostering:

1. the rights of species that depend on a healthy Salish Sea, including forage fish, salmon, and orca whales,
2. a healthy climate by moving away from fossil fuels, and
3. the overall health of the Salish Sea by reducing risks from oil spills, maintaining and expanding healthy shorelines, and keeping human-made noise to a minimum.

It wasn't all that long ago that communities started taking legal action to achieve goals similar to those of CRSJI. In 2006, Tamaqua Borough, Pennsylvania, banned dumping toxic sewage sludge as a violation of the Rights of Nature. Tamaqua was the very first place in the world to include the Rights of Nature in law. Since then, towns, cities, counties, states, and nations around the world—over one hundred municipalities so far—have been working to put protection of nature into law.

For example, in 2008, Ecuador became the first country in the world to recognize the Rights of Nature in its national constitution.

Three years later, the first Rights of Nature court decision was issued to repair and restore Ecuador's Vilcabamba River following damage from a highway-widening project.

In 2010, Pittsburgh became the first large U.S. city to enact a local law recognizing the Rights of Nature. The measure received a unanimous vote of the city council, following strong community organizing to support the measure. Toledo, Ohio, residents adopted the Lake Erie Bill of Rights in 2019, following three years of work for the right to vote on the measure. It's the first law in the U.S. to secure legal rights of a specific ecosystem. The following year, for the first time in U.S. history, the rights of a specific ecosystem were argued in federal court to defend the Lake Erie Bill of Rights. And in 2020, the Nez Perce Tribe General Council passed a resolution recognizing the Snake River as a living entity that has rights, including the right to exist, flourish, evolve, flow, regenerate—and a right to its restoration.

Locally, here's where things get really radical. The Rights of Nature would use San Juan County's legal system to:

- recognize the Salish Sea, including all its constituent ecosystems, communities, and native species as a living being and an entity with its own legal rights;
- define the rights of the Salish Sea;
- recognize the fundamental rights of First Nations and Tribal Nations Peoples to defend the Rights of the Salish Sea and to carry out their rights and obligations to protect the Salish Sea as traditional owners and custodians;
- prohibit actions that violate the rights of the Salish Sea;
- start court proceedings in the name of the Salish Sea;
- use the Rights of the Salish Sea as a tool to work with San Juan County and Washington State governments and state organizations to better protect the Salish Sea;
- reverse the onus of proof—when a person or community takes action to enforce the rights of the Salish Sea, laws

would require the development proponents to prove their project, activity, or development does not interfere with the rights of the Salish Sea;

- ensure, in cases of environmental destruction, that monetary damages derived from proceedings are used solely to restore the Salish Sea to its prior natural state.

Many CRSJI members believe the Home Rule Charter is basically the county's constitution. Like the U.S. constitution, a local one should have a Bill of Rights, ideally a universal one that includes nature. Some of the rights adopted by various cities and counties include rights to clean air, water, and soil; the rights of rivers, streams, and aquifers to exist, flourish, and naturally evolve; the right to a sustainable energy future, including freedom from activities related to fossil fuel extraction and production.

This work isn't for the faint of heart nor those seeking rapid change. Many communities have labored for decades, all the while facing harsh backlash from corporate and state interests. Some elected officials and other leaders working to protect the Salish Sea offer advice to sustain commitment:

- Be inspired, be aware, and don't feel bad you can't do everything.
- Don't succumb to analysis paralysis.
- Appreciate the quality of life you have and opportunities to speak up for species of the Salish Sea who don't have a voice.
- Get organized and raise hell.
- Do whatever you love doing and that inspires you.

The Home Rule charter revision commission has only one year to offer recommendations for changes to the document. Even if a Bill of Rights is accepted, there undoubtedly will be challenges to any and all laws CRSJI and allies try to enact. But trying is the least we can do to help the Salish Sea, and all its inhabitants, survive and thrive.

LIGHTS, CAMERA, ACTION

In film-making, nothing really happens until the director calls, "Action!" Well, that's not quite accurate; there's plenty that happens behind the scenes to get ready for the camera to roll. But the action, the filming on camera, is what everyone looks to in this art form.

The metaphor applies when it comes to protecting the Salish Sea from toxic wastes, restoring Chinook salmon populations, and removing threats to endangered Southern Resident whales. We need to take action for the sea to survive the effects of the climate crisis. To continue in the vernacular of the movie set, success requires many "takes," especially with difficult technical elements. If director Stanley Kubrick needed 127 takes for a scene in "The Shining," it's likely the complexity of a changing climate will require many kinds of action to heal the earth. Here are a few to consider, no matter where you live or what nature surrounds you.

TAKE 1: Learn all you can, however you can, about nearby rivers, streams, wetlands, and wildlife that need care and restoration.

TAKE 2: Speak for nature by writing letters and presenting testimony to elected officials, policy-makers, and other leaders with authority to create and change laws.

TAKE 3: Rally for climate justice and protest injustice when you see the effects of negligence and destruction on the earth.

TAKE 4: Don't eat Chinook salmon; leave them for the orcas to help them take in the calories they need to thrive.

TAKE 5: Donate time, money, talents, and/or expertise to the growing numbers of initiatives and organizations working to restore and renew threatened places and species.

TAKE 6: Vow to make your home and vehicle/s as free from harm to the environment as possible. This includes avoiding the use of toxic pesticides and fertilizers, repairing family vehicles to prevent leaks that end up in storm-water and eventually empty into bodies of water, reusing, and recycling.

TAKE 7: Find out which Indigenous Peoples lived in the place you call home. If you can, learn about them and their beliefs in their own words, teachings, art, music, and dance. Acknowledge their presence and welcome them home, remembering their ancestors lived there for time immemorial and likely didn't leave willingly.

TAKE 8: Go outdoors in all seasons and all types of weather. Smell, taste, touch, watch, and listen to the natural world around you.

There's no doubt we need to best Kubrick's record of takes in his films with our actions to save the Salish Sea and its endangered inhabitants. But, have you ever noticed the number of names that scroll down the screen at the end of a movie? Dozens to hundreds of them attest to the reality that no one does this work alone. Find your crew to keep the lights, camera, and action rolling.

YOUTH TAKE ON
THE GOVERNMENT

Look at one of the first pages in this collection and you'll see a dedication: For Maggie. That would be Margaret Katherine Graville Bricker. As I write this essay, she's just turned three and lives with her parents (my son and his wife) in Chicago. Maggie, and her generation, are a big part of what motivates me to work to save orcas, the Salish Sea, and the planet. At three, my granddaughter can't yet speak for the earth. But lots of other kids are doing that for her.

In August 2015, twenty-one young people, ages eight to nineteen, filed a lawsuit against the federal government. The lead plaintiff, Kelsey Juliana, was an environmental studies student at the University of Oregon in the case named *Juliana v. United States*; the youngest, eight-year-old Levi Draheim, was from a barrier island in Florida. Many of the plaintiffs, like Levi, were driven by first-hand experience of wildfires, hurricanes, floods, and other natural disasters that threatened them and their families.

The suit, filed in the U.S. District Court for the District of Oregon by the nonprofit law firm, Our Children's Trust, accused President Obama and the Federal Government of "violating Plaintiffs' fundamental constitutional rights to life, liberty, and property by substantially causing or contributing to a dangerous concentration of CO₂ in the atmosphere." It demanded the President implement a national plan to significantly reduce atmospheric concentrations of carbon dioxide by the year 2100. As the case spans across changing administrations, the current President becomes the named defendant, with the case currently naming the Biden Administration.

Something the plaintiffs and their legal team, led by Julia Olson, have experienced since the lawsuit filing is the roller coaster ride of suing the U.S. government: numerous motions by the defendants to dismiss the case, denial of motions to dismiss, and the filing of more motions, cancellation of trial dates and setting of new trial dates, petitions for new judges to hear the case, and dozens of "friends of the court" briefs in support of the plaintiffs. In March 2021, Our Children's Trust asked to amend the plaintiffs' original complaint. The amendment calls for the presentation of evidence in open court about how the nation's fossil fuel-based energy system is unconstitutional. Kelsey, Levi, and the other twenty-one youth plaintiffs await a ruling on the latest amendment from US District Court Judge Ann Aiken.

Attorneys and the plaintiffs are prepared to take their case to the U.S. Supreme Court. They've also asked to meet with the Department of Justice to discuss settlement options to protect the youths' fundamental rights.

According to the suit's lawyers, *Juliana v. United States* is similar to *Brown v. Board of Education* in 1954. That case succeeded at presenting evidence that segregated schools were unconstitutional. Our Children's Trust believes the first and most important step in constitutional cases is the declaration of rights and wrongs. "That's the driver of everything that follows."

I first heard of the youth's lawsuit from Liz Smith, my successor as the writer-in-residence on the Interisland ferry. In her application for the position, Liz listed one of her current projects—co-producer and archival researcher for a feature documentary film, *YOUTH V GOV*. I learned later that Liz's research work included reviewing hundreds of hours of archival clips of every president from Carter through Obama in which they called on the nation to leave the world a better place for future generations. Director Christi Cooper and the team also filmed over two hundred hours of original footage, including stories of the plaintiffs.

The *YOUTH V GOV* website claims the resulting two-hour feature film demonstrates that "In effect, the government has for decades made the world a better place for the fossil fuel industry." Once the first motion to dismiss the case was denied, Cooper felt it was time to present the story more widely, even though the suit was far from settled. "The climate crisis is affecting everyone, everywhere," Cooper says, "but as we know, those most affected are the vulnerable among us. It's important for viewers to see this reality at the heart of our democracy, and to also see how youth of all backgrounds are standing up to fight for their rights and their future."

Following its world premiere in November 2020 at the DOC NYC Film Festival, the documentary is making the rounds of film festivals around the U.S. It was selected as the Big Sky Centerpiece Film for the Big Sky Documentary Film Fest in February 2021 and was the opening night film at the DC Environmental Film Festival the following month.

⸻

During a recent Zoom call with Maggie, she showed her gramps and me how she arranged a row of chairs to help her step up on a table. I won't be surprised if, by the time she's a teenager, Maggie also steps up to take on the government.

RESOURCES

for further reading, listening, viewing, and action

BOOKS

Benedict, Audrey DeLella and Joseph K. Gaydos. *The Salish Sea – Jewel of the Pacific Northwest.* Seattle: Sasquatch Books, 2015.

Black, Martha and Lorne Hammond, Gavin Hanke with Nikki Sanchez, ed. *Spirits of the Coast: Orcas in Science, Art, and History.* Victoria: Royal British Columbia Museum, 2020.

Carson, Rachel. *The Sea Around Us.* Oxford: Oxford University Press, 1951.

Carson, Rachel. *Silent Spring.* New York: Houghton Mifflin, 1962.

Demar, Robert E. and Robin Atkins. *Nautical Highways: Ferries of the San Juan Islands.* Friday Harbor: Tiger Press & Rain Barrel Productions, 2002.

Gaydos, Joseph K. and Audrey DeLella Benedict. *Explore the Salish Sea: A Nature Guide for Kids.* Seattle: Little Bigfoot, 2018.

Fylling, Marni. *Fylling's Illustrated Guide to Pacific Coast Tide Pools.* Berkeley: Heyday, 2015.

Jacobsen, Rowan. *The Living Shore: Rediscovering a Lost World.* New York: Bloomsbury, 2009.

Kruckeberg, Arthur R. *The Natural History of Puget Sound Country.* Seattle: University of Washington Press, 1991.

Lear, Linda, ed. *Lost Woods: The Discovered Writing of Rachel Carson.* Boston: Beacon Press, 1998.

Lopez, Barry, ed. *The Future of Nature: Writing on a Human Ecology from Orion Magazine.* Minneapolis: Milkweed Editions, 2007.

Macy, Joanna and Chris Johnstone. *Active Hope: How to Face the Mess We're in without Going Crazy.* Novato: New World Library, 2012.

Mapes, Lynda V. *Orca: Shared Waters, Shared Home.* Seattle: Braided River and *The Seattle Times,* 2021.

McBride, Andrew Shattuck, and Jill McCabe Johnson, editors. *For Love of Orcas: An Anthology.* Eastound: Wandering Aengus Press, 2019.

Moore, Kathleen Dean. *Great Tide Rising: Towards Clarity and Moral Courage in a Time of Planetary Change.* Berkeley: Counterpoint, 2016.

Morton, Alexandra. *Listening to Whales: What the Orcas Have Taught Us.* New York: Random House Publishing Group, 2008.

Osborne, Richard, John Calambokidis, and Eleanor M. Dorsey. *A Guide to Marine Mammals of Greater Puget Sound.* Anacortes: Island Publishers, 1988.

Pratt, Boyd C. *Lime: Quarrying and Limemaking in the San Juan Islands.* Friday Harbor: Mulno Cove Publishing, 2016.

Shields, Monika Wieland. *Endangered Orcas: The Story of the Southern Residents.* Friday Harbor: Orca Watcher, 2019.

Sideris, Lisa H. and Kathleen Dean Moore, ed. *Rachel Carson: Legacy and Challenge.* Albany: State University of New York, 2008.

Thunberg, Greta. *No One is Too Small to Make a Difference.* UK: Penguin Random House, 2019.

Vernon, Susan, illustrations by Nancy McDonnell Spaulding. *Rainshadow World: A Naturalist's Year in the San Juan Islands.* Friday Harbor: Archipelago Press, 2010.

Yunker, John, ed. *Writing for Animals: New Perspectives for Writers and Instructors to Educate and Inspire.* Ashland, OR: Ashland Creek Press, 2018.

"An Inconvenient Truth." Director Davis Guggenheim weaves the science of global warming with former Vice President Al Gore's personal history and lifelong commitment to reversing the effects of global climate change. 2006. www.algore.com/library/an-inconvenient-truth-dvd

"An Inconvenient Sequel: Truth to Power." Follow-up to "An Inconvenient Truth" that shows just how close we are to a real energy revolution. 2017. www.algore.com/library/an-inconvenient-sequel-truth-to-power

"Dismantled." Podcast for intersectional environmentalists plus voices focused on climate justice. www.intersectionalenvironmentalist.com/dismantled-podcast

"Mothers of Invention." Podcast on feminist climate change solutions from (mostly) women around the world. Hosted by Mary Robinson, first female President of Ireland; Maeve Higgins, comedian-writer based in New York City; and Thimali Kodikara, series producer. www.mothersofinvention.online/episodes

"Salish Sea Wild." Adventure videos of the Salish Sea's ecosystem with wildlife veterinarian Joe Gaydos and Team SeaDoc. www.youtube.com/watch?v=oDI1QmvN3j8

YOUTH V GOV. This film is the story of twenty-one plaintiffs, now ages 13 to 24, who have been suing the U.S. government since 2015 for its willful actions in creating the climate crisis the youth will inherit. www.youthvgovthefilm.com

List of favorite 2020 climate podcasts from "Grist," a nonprofit, independent media organization dedicated to telling stories of climate solutions and a just future: grist.org/fix/2020-was-the-year-climate-podcasts-went-mainstream-here-are-our-favorites/

All We Can Save Project
Building power and joy to support women leading on climate
and to nurture a just and livable future.
www.allwecansave.earth

American Cetacean Society
Founded in 1967; the oldest whale, dolphin, and porpoise
conservation group in the world.
www.acsonline.org

Center for Whale Research
Since 1976, CWR has studied Southern Resident killer whales in
the Salish Sea. CWR performs health assessments to ensure the
viability of the whale population, informs elected officials of their
ecosystem needs, and shares the whales' story with the world.
www.whaleresearch.com/mission

Community Rights San Juan Islands
A Washington State non-profit working to recognize in law
the rights of the Salish Sea to exist, thrive, and regenerate vital
lifecycles. Rights of Nature is a legal framework to bridge ancient
recognition of our human place in the web of life and our
modern legal system, to shift our view of nature as property, to
one that recognizes and respects nature as rights bearing.
www.rightsofthesalishsea.org

Friends of the San Juans
Citizen group formed in 1979 to protect and restore the San Juan
Islands and the Salish Sea. Efforts include education; advocacy;
citizen engagement;habitat restoration; and protection of water,
forest, farmland and endangered species.
www.sanjuans.org

Intersectional Environmentalist
Intersectional environmentalism is an inclusive form of
environmentalism that advocates for the protection
of all people and the planet.
www.intersectionalenvironmentalist.com/about-ie

Orca Network
Non-profit organization dedicated to raising awareness of the
whales of the Pacific Northwest, and the importance of providing
them healthy and safe habitats.
www.orcanetwork.org

Save Our Wild Salmon
A diverse, nationwide coalition working to restore
wild salmon and steelhead to the rivers, streams, and marine
waters of the Pacific Northwest for the benefit of the region's
ecology, economy, and culture.
www.wildsalmon.org

SeaDoc Society
Founded in 2000, the SeaDoc Society conducts and sponsors
scientific research in the inland waters of the Pacific Northwest
and translates science into action.
www.seadocsociety.org/about

The Whale Museum
Promotes stewardship of whales and the Salish Sea
ecosystem through education and research.
www.whalemuseum.org

Wild Orca
Working since 2014 to engage the public and policymakers to
recover Southern Resident killer whales.
https://www.wildorca.org

ACKNOWLEDGMENTS

Some of the essays in this collection have been published previously. Many thanks to the editors who have included them.

"Salish Sea Account." Essay included in the anthology *For the Love of Orcas*. Wandering Aengus Press, 2019.

"Not Just a Drill." Essay included in the anthology *The Madrona Project Issue #2*. Empty Bowl, 2021

"Environmentalism Meets Anti-Racism." *Wayfarer Magazine*. Homebound Publications, Spring 2021.

"Nine Ways to Write When You're the Writer-in-Residence on the Washington State Ferry." *Brevity's* Nonfiction Blog. November 17, 2021.

THANK YOU

I still don't have a life vest with WRITER written on the chest, but I'm constantly buoyed by an extensive fleet of family, friends (writers and non-writers), teachers, and sea life. Some essayists, myself included, like the list form to achieve concision when there's lots of ground to cover. Here's my list of thank yous to my companions on this journey.

To Leslie M. Browning, poet, novelist, photographer, book designer, editor and founder of Homebound Publications for offering a home for my writing, for making sure "the mainstream isn't the only stream," for creating a community of writers I treasure, and for friendship.

To the Women Writers of the Salish Sea. We joined together over twenty years ago, meeting one morning, every other week. Then we switched to Thursday afternoons, every week, and called ourselves the Thursday Writers. A few years ago, we agreed we needed a better name and chose Women Writers of the Salish Sea, or WWSS. We still meet every Thursday, even during a pandemic (by Zoom), to critique each other's writing and offer other support. A few members have left, a few have died, some have left and returned, and new women have joined. The WWSS has seen me through two books of profiles, a memoir, and this essay collection. I know my writing is better for their questions and suggestions.

To the Red House Writers for encouragement when I initially thought creating a writing residency on a state ferry was a wacky idea. And to Sue Roundy for that wacky idea.

To the Washington State Ferries System for welcoming my request for a writing residency on the Interisland; former ferry captain Ken Bertness for not laughing at the residency idea and steering me to the right contact; and the entire crew of the MV *Tillikum*.

To former Washington State Poet Laureate Elizabeth Austen and former Oregon State Poet Laureate Kim Stafford for help to think and write more poetically; writers and teachers Ana Maria Spagna and Laura Pritchett for help to think more creatively about prose.

To the many champions of the Salish Sea and Southern Resident orcas including Joseph K. Gaydos and the SeaDoc Society; Debra Giles and the Canine Conservation Program; Jenny Atkinson and Tracie Merrill of The Whale Museum and the Marine Naturalist Training Program; The Whiteley Center at Friday Harbor Labs; Lovell Pratt and the Friends of the San Juans; The Center for Whale Research; Lynda Mapes, *Seattle Times* environment reporter; and Community Rights San Juan Islands.

To Lopez Island Friends Meeting for spiritual grounding and help with discernment.

To the Southern Residents for teaching me about community, grief, and the importance of traveling in pods.

To Rae, Matthew, Jenn, and Maggie, my lights now and into the future.

To Jerry for everything, always.

ABOUT THE AUTHOR

Iris Graville has lived in Washington State for four decades, after childhood and early adulthood in Chicago and small towns in Southern Illinois and Indiana. A long-time Quaker, an environmental and anti-racism activist, and a retired nurse, Iris believes everyone has a story to tell. She's the author of two collections of profiles—*Hands at Work* and BOUNTY: *Lopez Island Farmers, Food, and Community.* Her memoir, *Hiking Naked,* was a 2019 recipient of a Nautilus Award.

Iris holds a Master of Nursing degree from the University of Washington; she focused most of her nursing career in public health. She also pursued her early love of writing, and in 2015, Iris earned a Master of Fine Arts in Creative Writing from the Northwest Institute of Literary Arts.

Her writing has appeared in journals and anthologies, and she's been nominated for a Pushcart Prize. She's also publisher of *Sharkreef Literary Magazine,* a staff writer for *The Wayfarer Magazine,* and a Homebound Publications Advisory Board member.

In 2018, Iris was named the first Writer-in-Residence for the Washington State Ferries. Sometimes you'll still find her writing on the Interisland ferry as the vessel courses among the San Juan Islands.

Since 1996, Iris and her husband, a retired sign language interpreter, have lived on traditional Coast Salish lands, now called Lopez Island, Washington. They tend a large garden, ride bicycles, and walk the trails and beaches surrounding their home. They have two grown children and a grandchild. Learn more at irisgraville.com.

HOMEBOUND
PUBLICATIONS

We are an award-winning independent publisher founded in 2011 striving to ensure that the mainstream is not the only stream. More than a company, we are a community of writers and readers exploring the larger questions we face as a global village. It is our intention to preserve contemplative storytelling. We publish full-length introspective works of creative non-fiction, literary fiction, and poetry.

WWW.HOMEBOUNDPUBLICATIONS.COM